HOORAY for the USA!

Written by John and Patty Carratello

Illustrated by Sue Fullam and Theresa Wright

The classroom teacher may reproduce copies of materials in this book for classroom use only. The reproduction of any part for an entire school or school system is strictly prohibited. No part of this publication may be transmitted, stored, or recorded in any form without written permission from the publisher.

Teacher Created Materials, Inc.
P.O. Box 1214
Huntington Beach, CA 92647
© 1991 Teacher Created Materials, Inc.
Made in U.S.A.
ISBN 1-55734-113-3

Table of Contents

Introduction 3

Holidays:

Columbus Day 4
Veterans Day 9
Thanksgiving 15
New Year's Day 20
Martin Luther King, Jr.'s Birthday 24
Presidents' Day 29
Arbor Day 36
Mother's Day and Father's Day 40
Memorial Day 46
Flag Day 50
Independence Day 54
Labor Day 60

Symbols:

The United States Flag 66
Uncle Sam 72
The Liberty Bell 76
The Bald Eagle 80
The White House 85
The United States Capitol 91
The Statue of Liberty 94
Ellis Island 100
Famous Memorials 102
Mount Rushmore 109

Introduction

The history of the United States is rich with the people and events that have made it the great nation it is today—a nation filled with holidays and symbols which remind its citizens of its unique heritage and bring a swell of pride to the hearts and minds of freedom-loving patriots everywhere.

In *Hooray for the USA!*, children are introduced to the holidays and symbols of the United States. The history of each holiday and symbol is explained and a related project is provided.

Once this book has been introduced and enjoyed by your students, they too will say, "Hooray for the USA!"

Columbus Day

Columbus Day

On the second Monday of October each year, the people of the United States remember the explorer who led Europe to the Western Hemisphere in 1492. Because of this explorer's desire to find a shortcut to the riches of Asia, the New World was discovered. His name was Christopher Columbus.

Christopher Columbus approached King Ferdinand and Queen Isabella of Spain with a plan to reach the gold and spices of India. The riches from this country had been brought at great expense to Europe by overland caravans. Columbus reasoned that if he kept sailing west, he would eventually reach Asia and could avoid sailing around the tip of Africa. The King and Queen financed the voyage and promised Columbus honors and a percentage of the trade as well.

After sailing for three weeks without seeing land, Columbus and the crews aboard his three ships saw the land of the Bahamas. It was October 12, 1492. He named the first island they saw San Salvador.

Columbus returned to Spain with news of his discoveries, and opened the doors of trade and settlement between Europe and America.

Columbus Day

The First Voyage

Use reference material to map the route Columbus took on his first voyage across the Atlantic Ocean.

FIRST VOYAGE

August 3, 1492: Departure from Palos, Spain

October 12, 1492: Arrival at San Salvador

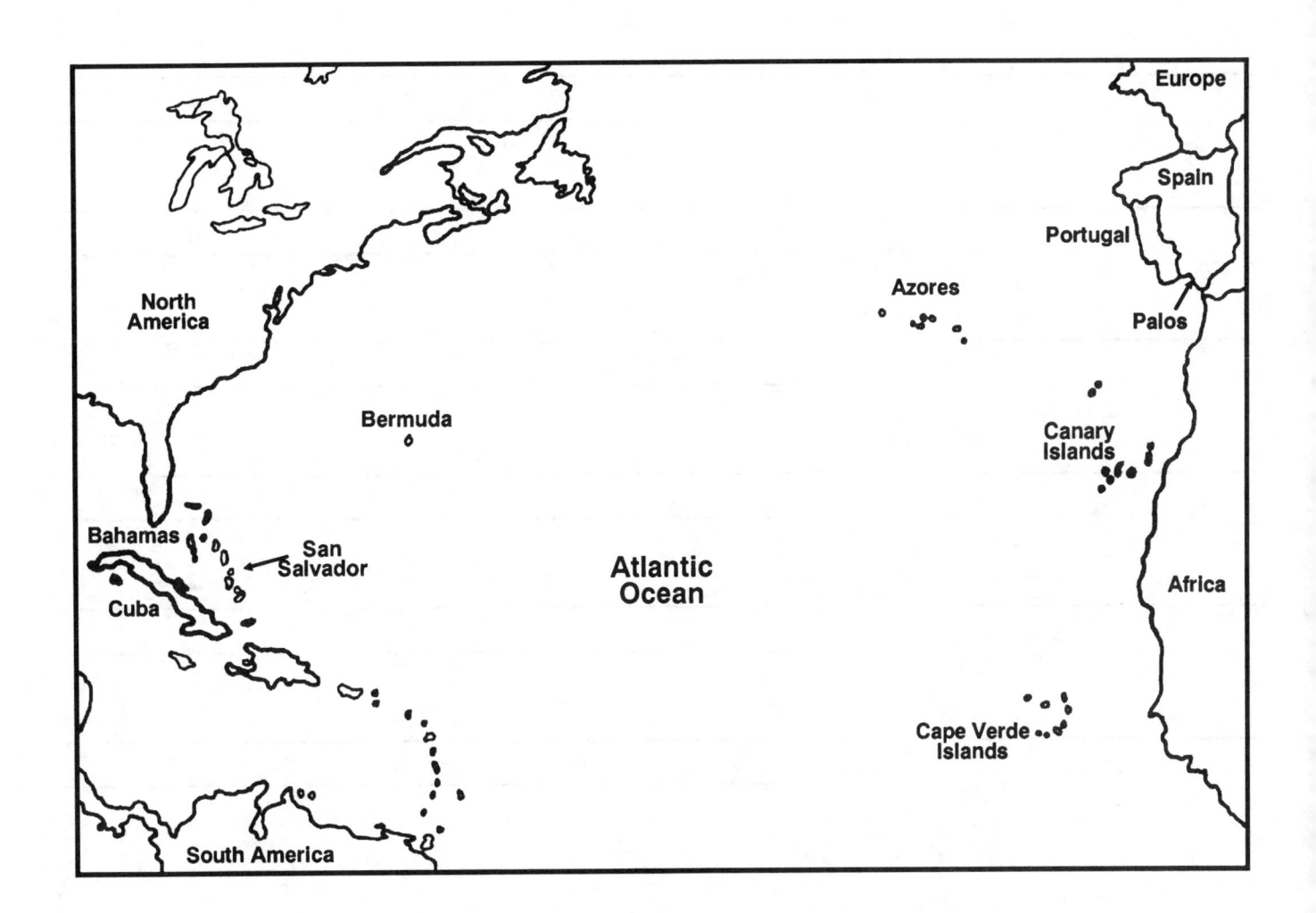

Columbus Day

The First Voyage (cont.)

Columbus and his crew had sailed for three weeks without seeing land, the longest anyone had ever been sailing in one direction without spotting land. Needless to say, the crew was beginning to worry about the outcome of this voyage.

Working in a small group, write a dialogue between Columbus and several of his crew members as they begin to make their restlessness known. When you have finished your dialogue, perform it for the class.

_____ : _____
_____

_____ : _____
_____

_____ : _____
_____

_____ : _____
_____

_____ : _____
_____

_____ : _____
_____

_____ : _____
_____

#113 Hooray for the USA! © 1991 Teacher Created Materials, Inc.

Columbus Day

The First Voyage (cont.)

Although Christopher Columbus has often been recognized as the person to "discover" America, America was already inhabited by natives who had lived on the land for thousands of years.

Imagine that you and your classmates are the natives of "San Salvador," which Columbus has just discovered. Answer the questions below from what you suppose their viewpoint might have been.

1. How do you think the natives would have reacted to the sight of the *Niña*, the *Pinta*, and the *Santa Maria* docking on their island?

   _____
   _____

2. Would you welcome or fight the strangers to your land? Why?

   _____
   _____

3. What could you teach these new men and boys?

   _____
   _____

4. What could you learn from these travelers?

   _____
   _____

5. How could these people change your way of life?

   _____
   _____

6. Would you like to sail with them to their country? Why?

   _____
   _____

7. After getting to know them, do you want them to stay on your island or leave for home? Why?

   _____
   _____

Columbus Day

The First Voyage (cont.)

You are Christopher Columbus and you have just returned home from your history-making voyage. You have been asked to design a poster that would encourage trade and settlement in the lands you have discovered for Spain. King Ferdinand and Queen Isabella of Spain have agreed to pay you quite well for your advertisement.

Design your poster in the space provided on this page.

#113 Hooray for the USA! 8 © 1991 Teacher Created Materials, Inc.

Veterans Day

Veterans Day

Veterans Day is a day that honors those men and women who have served their country in the United States Armed Forces. November 11 is the day these special people are honored.

In our country, Veterans Day was not always known by that name. On November 11, 1918 (The 11th hour of the 11th day of the 11th month), World War I ended. This war was known as "The War to End All Wars" and people the world over rejoiced. The day became known as "Armistice Day" in honor of the truce of peace that was made on this day.

Armistice Day became a day to recognize those people who had fought so courageously in World War I and to celebrate the peace that now existed. November 11 was made a federal holiday in 1938. But shortly after this holiday was declared, World War II broke out. The dream of The War to End All Wars was now gone. Many lives were lost during this second world war, and those who lost loved ones and those who fought for their country needed to be recognized as well as those World War I patriots.

In 1954, Congress changed the name of Armistice Day to Veterans Day, in order to honor all United States Veterans. At this time, President Eisenhower asked all Americans to strive for peace.

In the United States, people remember Veterans Day with celebrations, parades, speeches, and special services. It is a day to honor all the veterans who have served the United States.

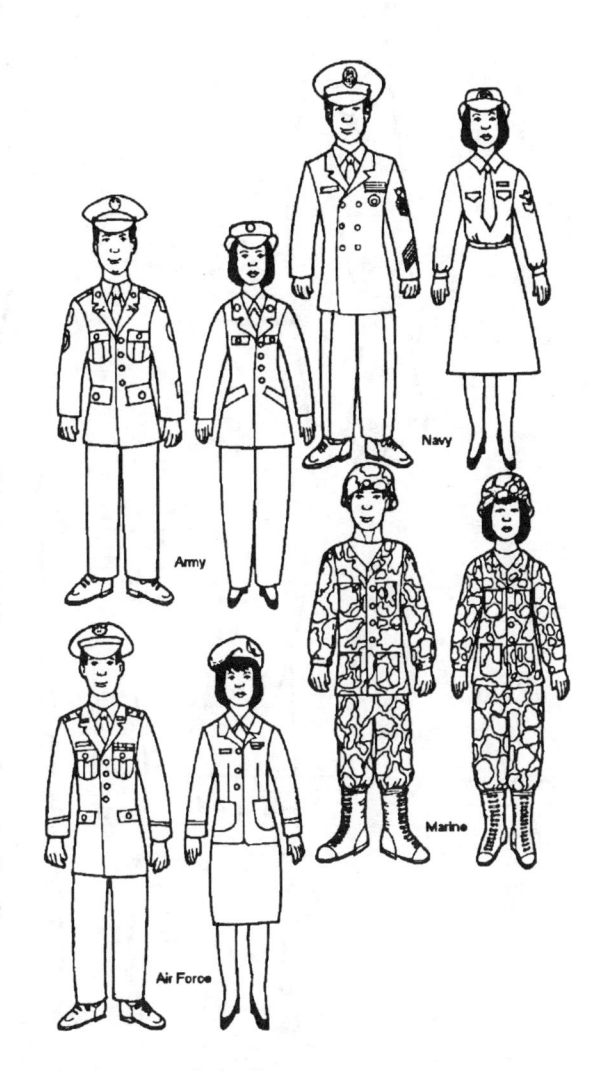

Veterans Day

The Figures

Here are a male and female figure you can use to display the uniforms (see pages 11-14) of various branches of the military service. Color and cut them out.

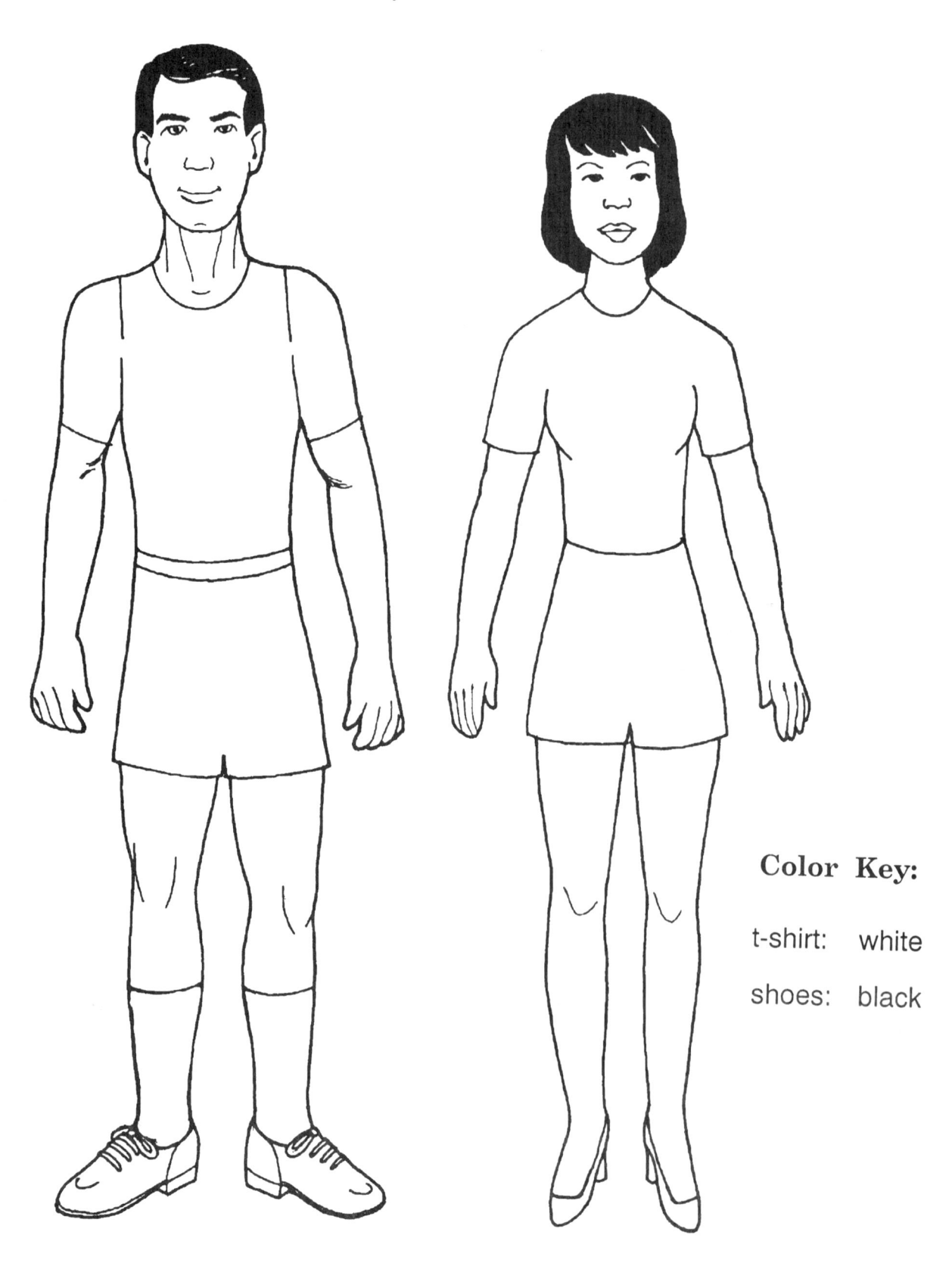

Color Key:

t-shirt: white

shoes: black

#113 Hooray for the USA! 10 © 1991 Teacher Created Materials, Inc.

Veterans Day

Army

Color and cut out these Army uniforms. Use them on the figures found on page 10 of this activity.

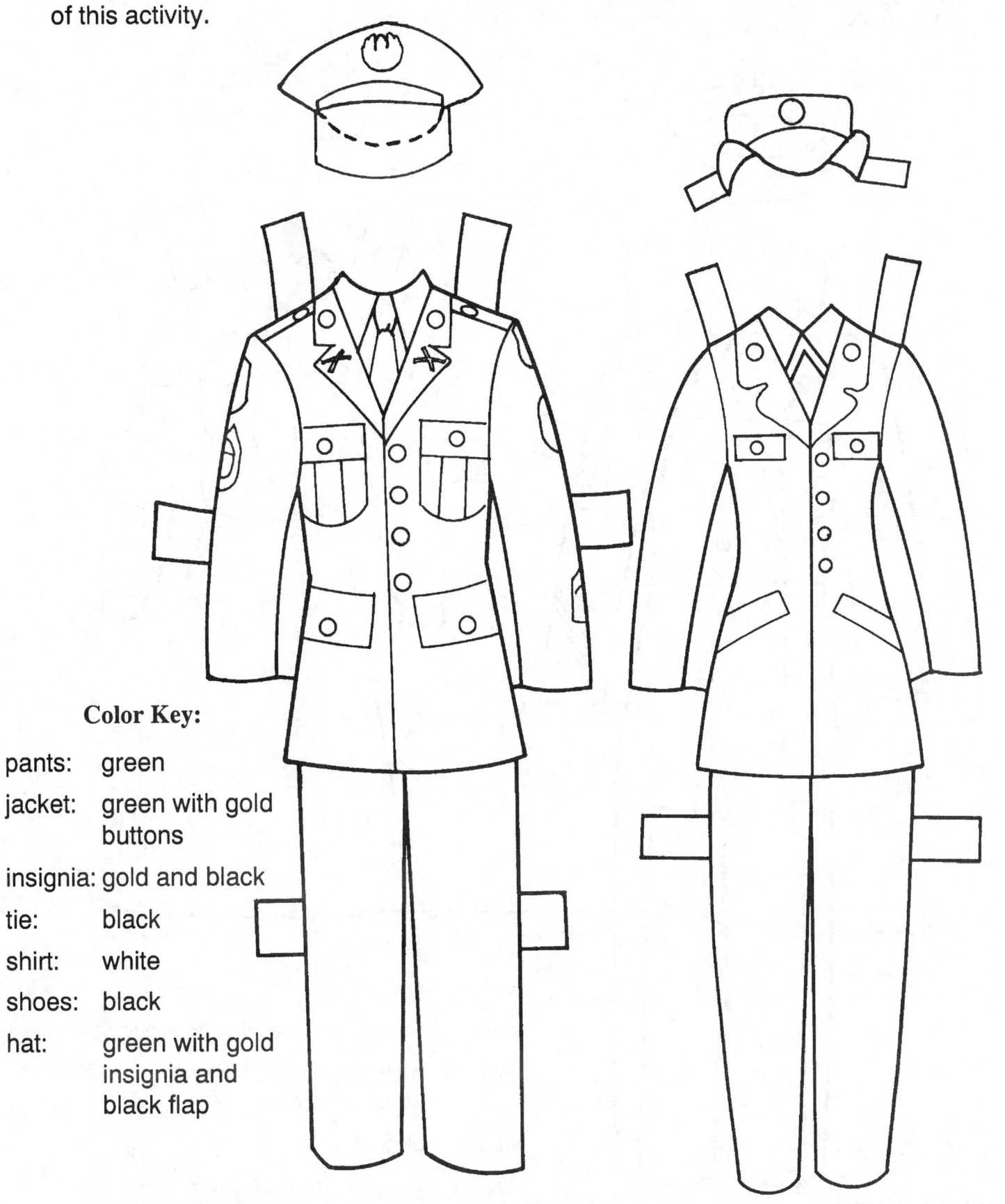

Color Key:

pants: green

jacket: green with gold buttons

insignia: gold and black

tie: black

shirt: white

shoes: black

hat: green with gold insignia and black flap

© 1991 Teacher Created Materials, Inc. #113 Hooray for the USA!

Veterans Day

Navy

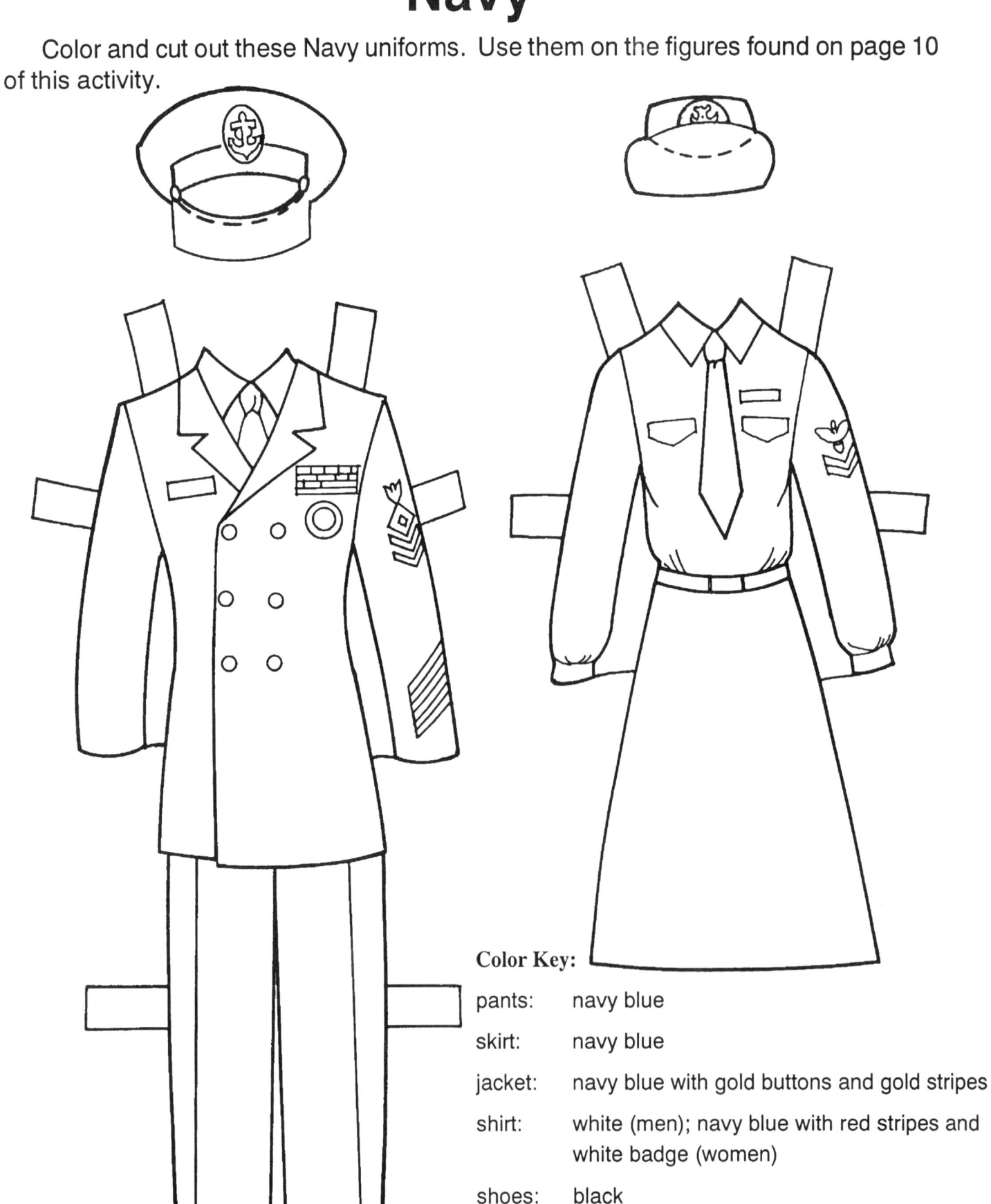

Color and cut out these Navy uniforms. Use them on the figures found on page 10 of this activity.

Color Key:

pants:	navy blue
skirt:	navy blue
jacket:	navy blue with gold buttons and gold stripes
shirt:	white (men); navy blue with red stripes and white badge (women)
shoes:	black
hat:	white with navy blue trim

#113 Hooray for the USA! © 1991 Teacher Created Materials, Inc.

Veterans Day

Air Force

Color and cut out these Air Force uniforms. Use them on the figures found on page 10 of this activity.

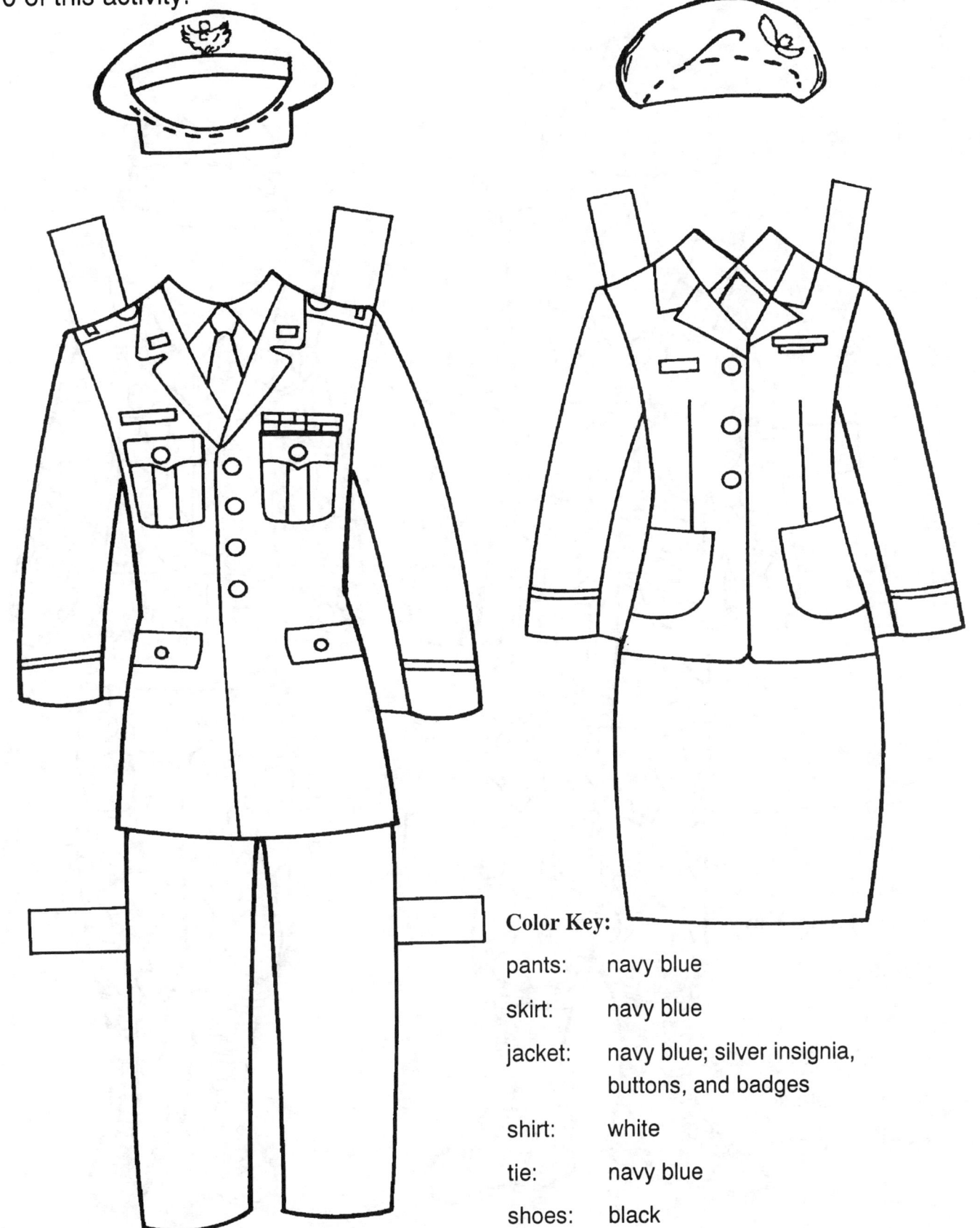

Color Key:

pants:	navy blue
skirt:	navy blue
jacket:	navy blue; silver insignia, buttons, and badges
shirt:	white
tie:	navy blue
shoes:	black

© 1991 Teacher Created Materials, Inc.   13   #113 Hooray for the USA!

Veterans Day

Marines

Color and cut out these Marine uniforms. Use them on the figures found on page 10 of this activity.

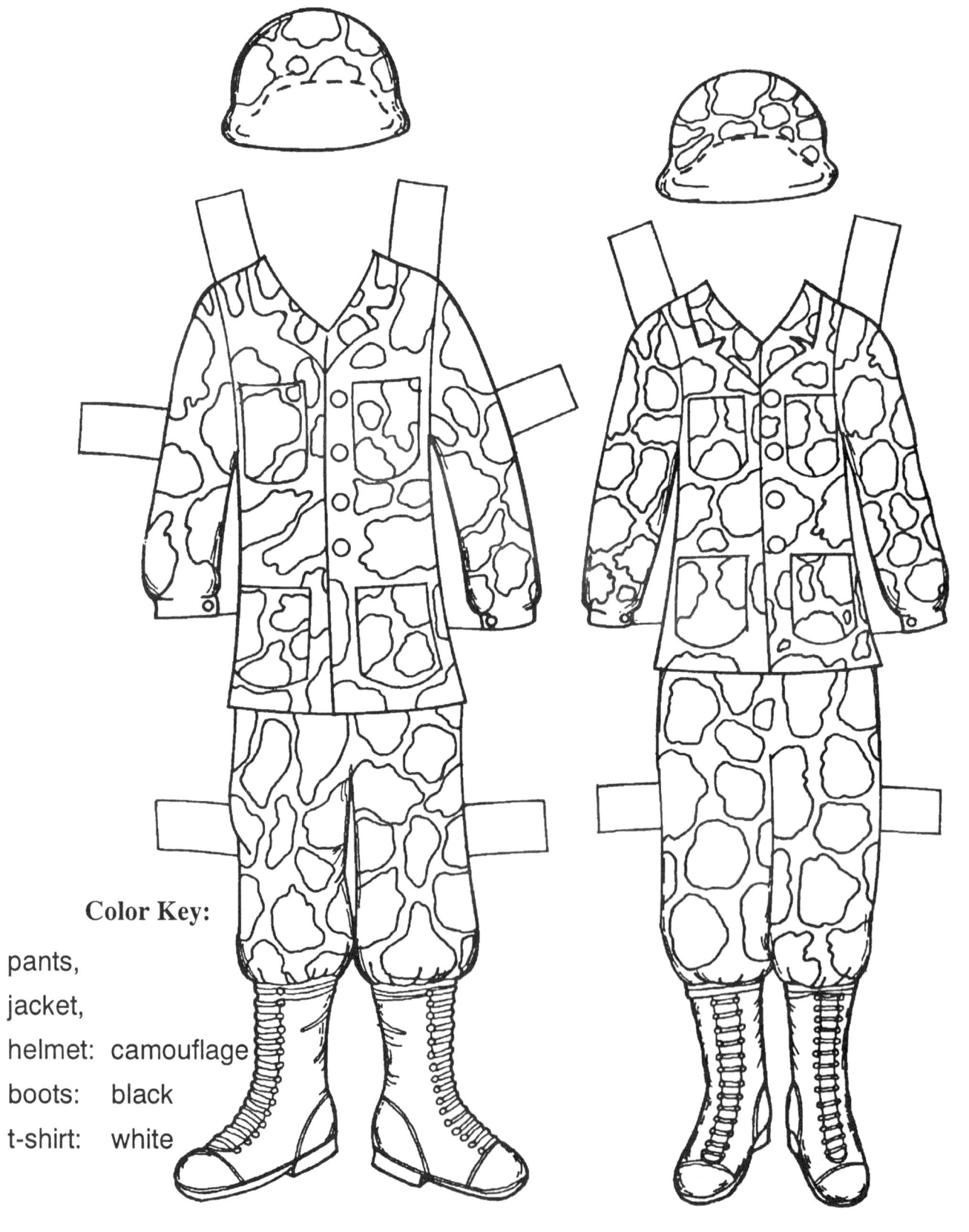

Color Key:

pants,
jacket,
helmet: camouflage
boots: black
t-shirt: white

#113 Hooray for the USA! © 1991 Teacher Created Materials, Inc.

Thanksgiving

Thanksgiving

Thanksgiving is a time when families join together to share in a holiday meal and show their love and appreciation for each other. The first Thanksgiving was no exception. This oldest holiday tradition in America began with a feast between Pilgrims and Indians in October, 1621.

In search of religious freedom and freedom from unfair laws, men and women left England on the *Mayflower*. They arrived in Plymouth, Massachusetts in 1620, ready to begin new lives in the New World.

The first year on American soil was a difficult one for the Pilgrims. But the Indians were friendly and helped the new settlers learn many ways to live off the land. In the fall of 1621, the Pilgrims' governor, William Bradford, decided that a celebration was due, an occasion to celebrate their harvest, their new Indian friends, and their joy at being alive.

Chief Massasoit, leader of the Wampanoags, and 90 of his men were invited to the first Thanksgiving feast. The celebration lasted three days. Here is a menu of some of the things they ate:

turkey	cornbread	biscuits	clams
deer	roasted corn	dried plums	watercress
leeks	cherries	gooseberries	fish
geese	ducks	lobsters	oysters
mince pie	pumpkin pie	sweet potatoes	cranberry sauce

The first Thanksgiving was a very successful celebration!

In 1789, George Washington made Thanksgiving Day a nationwide event for all 13 colonies. It was to be a day of rejoicing and giving thanks for the United States' victory over England in the Revolutionary War. In 1863, President Abraham Lincoln proclaimed the last Thursday in November as National Thanksgiving Day. Finally, in 1941 Congress set Thanksgiving day as the fourth Thursday in November.

© 1991 Teacher Created Materials, Inc.   #113 Hooray for the USA!

Thanksgiving

The Other Thanksgiving
A Play

Narrator: This is a story about the first Thanksgiving that the history books never tell. While the grownups were out making history at their Thanksgiving celebration, the Indian and Pilgrim boys and girls decided to have a celebration of their own.

Stage Directions

The Indian boys and girls are playing in the forest. The boys are watching two of the boys wrestle, and the girls are playing a string game, cats-in-the-cradle.

The Pilgrim children enter stage left.

The Indian boys stop wrestling and the girls stop their game. They watch quietly as the strangers approach.

Indian Boy 1: (In a stage whisper) Look, it's the children from the Pilgrim tribe!

Indian Boy 2: (Also in a stage whisper) I wonder what they want?

Thanksgiving

The Other Thanksgiving (cont.)

Stage Directions

The Pilgrim children notice the Indian children.

Pilgrim Girl 1: (Stage whisper) I'm scared. They look dangerous to me.

Pilgrim Boy 1: (Stage whisper) That may be so, but Father told us that we must make friends with the Indians.

Pilgrim Girl 2: Okay, but. . .

Pilgrim Boy 2: But what if they know we're scared?

Pilgrim Boy 1: They won't if you just be quiet and let me do the talking.

Stage Directions

Pilgrim Girl 1, *Pilgrim Girl 2*, and *Pilgrim Boy 2*, get into a conference huddle—each takes a turn looking up from the huddle at the Indians, who are quietly looking on. The three finally turn to *Pilgrim Boy 1* all at once and speak in frightened consensus.

Pilgrim Girl 1,
Pilgrim Girl 2, and
Pilgrim Boy 2: (In unison), O-KAY!

Pilgrim Boy 1: Okay, follow me.

Stage Directions

Pilgrim Boy 1 must keep coaxing the other three along. It takes him quite awhile to get across the stage area to where the Indian children are talking. Meanwhile . . .

Indian Girl 1: (Stage whisper) I'm scared. They look dangerous to me.

Indian Boy 3: (Stage whisper) That may be so, but Father told us that we must make friends with the Pilgrims.

Indian Girl 2: Okay, but . . .

Indian Boy 4: But what if they know we're scared?

Indian Boy 3: They won't if you just be quiet and let me do the talking.

Thanksgiving

The Other Thanksgiving (cont.)

Stage Directions

Indian Girl 1, Indian Girl 2, And Indian Boy 4 get into a conference huddle—each takes a turn looking up from the huddle at the Pilgrims, who are making their way across the stage. The three finally turn to *Indian Boy 3* all at once, in frightened consensus.

Indian Girl 1,
Indian Girl 2, and
Indian Boy 4:   (In unison), O-KAY!

Indian Boy 3:   Okay, follow me.

Stage Directions

The two groups walk toward each other, stopping when there is a distance of about three feet between them. At first they just stand there, staring cautiously. Then, finally, *Pilgrim Boy 1* and *Indian Boy 3* walk forward and . . .

Indian Boy 3:   Hi!

Pilgrim Boy 1:   Glad to meet you. We have come to make friends.

Indian Boy 3:   Sounds good to me. People can always use more friends. Would you like to play with us?

Pilgrim Girl 3:   (Finding enough courage to come forward) Yes. That sounds terrific!

Indian Girl 1:   Would you like to play chase around the tree?

Indian Girl 3:   One person says, "Okay, I'm going to catch you."

Indian Boy 1:   And then he chases that person until he catches him . . .

Indian Boy 2:   . . . or until the person he is chasing can run to a place where the chaser cannot get him.

Pilgrim Boy 3:   Oh, we call that game Tag!

Everyone: (Not in unison) That sounds good, let's play. Yeah, let's play. It'll be fun.

Pilgrim Boy 4:   I'll be "It"!

Thanksgiving

The Other Thanksgiving (cont.)

Stage Directions

Everyone plays tag for about 10 seconds. Everyone is having a good time—laughing, running. Then, finally . . .

Pilgrim Girl 4: (Out of breath) That was fun!

Everyone: (Not in unison) Yes. That was fun. We should do it again soon.

Indian Girl 1: We have brought food—dried plums and cherries. Would you like to share it with us?

Pilgrim Boy 5: Yes we would. But we have brought food as well. Let us have a feast!

Indian Boy 3: A feast of . . . of . . .

Pilgrim Girl 1: Thanksgiving. We shall call it Thanksgiving.

Indian Boy 3: Thanks for our friends.

Everyone: (Affirmations, like, "Yes; All right"; etc.)

Pilgrim Boy 2: . . . for good food.

Everyone: (Affirmations, like, "Yes; All right"; etc.)

Indian Girl 3: . . . for everything we can learn from each other.

Everyone: (Affirmations, like, "Yes; All right"; etc.)

Stage Directions

Food is distributed, while everyone talks (stage talk). Then everyone faces the audience.

Everyone: (In unison) HAPPY THANKSGIVING!

New Year's Day

New Year's Day

The first day of the new year is a day full of hope and promise, a day when people throughout the country and throughout the world reflect, celebrate, and look forward to new beginnings.

New Year's Day is the first day of each calendar year. In the United States, many people get ready to welcome the new year with a festive New Year's Eve party. At 12 o'clock midnight bells ring noisily, firecrackers pop, people embrace, and shouts of "Happy New Year!" fill the air. On New Year's Day, Americans often enjoy watching parades and football games and visiting with their family and friends.

New Year's Day is a day of celebration!

New Year's Day

Let's Have a Parade!

Float decorations and parades are a big part of New Year's Day celebrations for many Americans. Now's your chance to join in the fun!

You and your classmates will be making your own floats for a New Year's Day Classroom Parade. Each person will be responsible for the design and construction of his or her own float. You may wish to select a theme for your parade floats, or allow each student to create a float related to an individually chosen theme. Here are some ideas:

"Great Moments in American History"

"Animals, Animals, Animals!"

"Creatures of the Imagination"

"Symbols of America"

"Kids' Stuff"

"Our World of the Future"

"Parade of Colors"

"In the Day of the Dinosaurs"

"Toys on Parade"

These are just a few theme ideas you can use. Think of some more themes and write them here.

_____

_____

After you have chosen a theme for your float or for all the floats in the parade, begin your designing.

Here are the materials you will need to make your float:

- 2 empty thread spools that are the same size and shape
- 2 plastic drinking straws
- 1 individual serving size cereal box, 1 milk carton, half of an egg carton, or similar size containers
- yarn or string
- materials for decoration, as desired

To make your float, follow the directions on pages 22 - 23.

New Year's Day

Let's Have a Parade! (cont.)

1. Decorate your small box or carton according to the theme you have chosen.

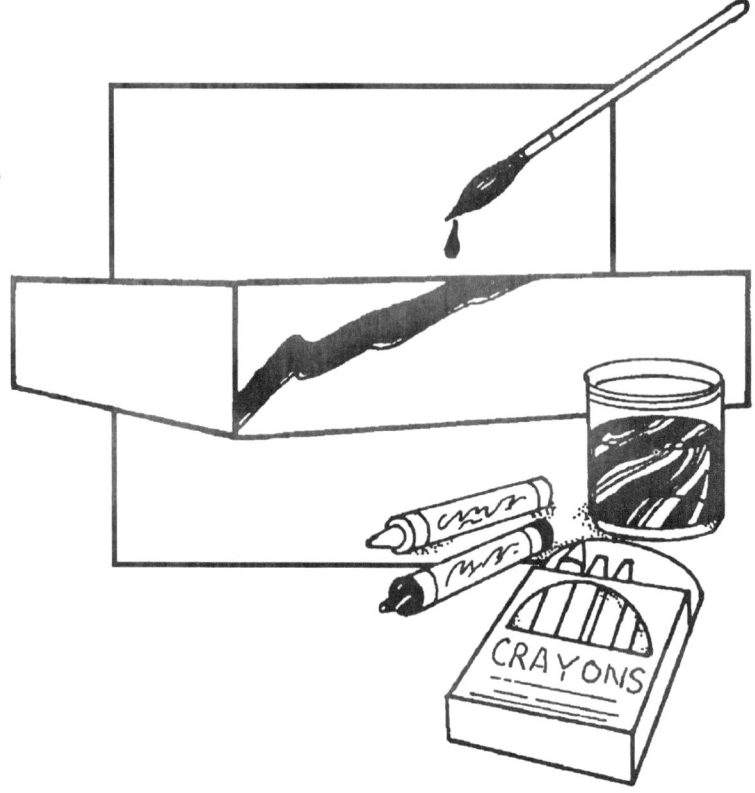

Be sure your decorations do not hang down too far below the bottom of the float. Remember, your float will have "wheels!"

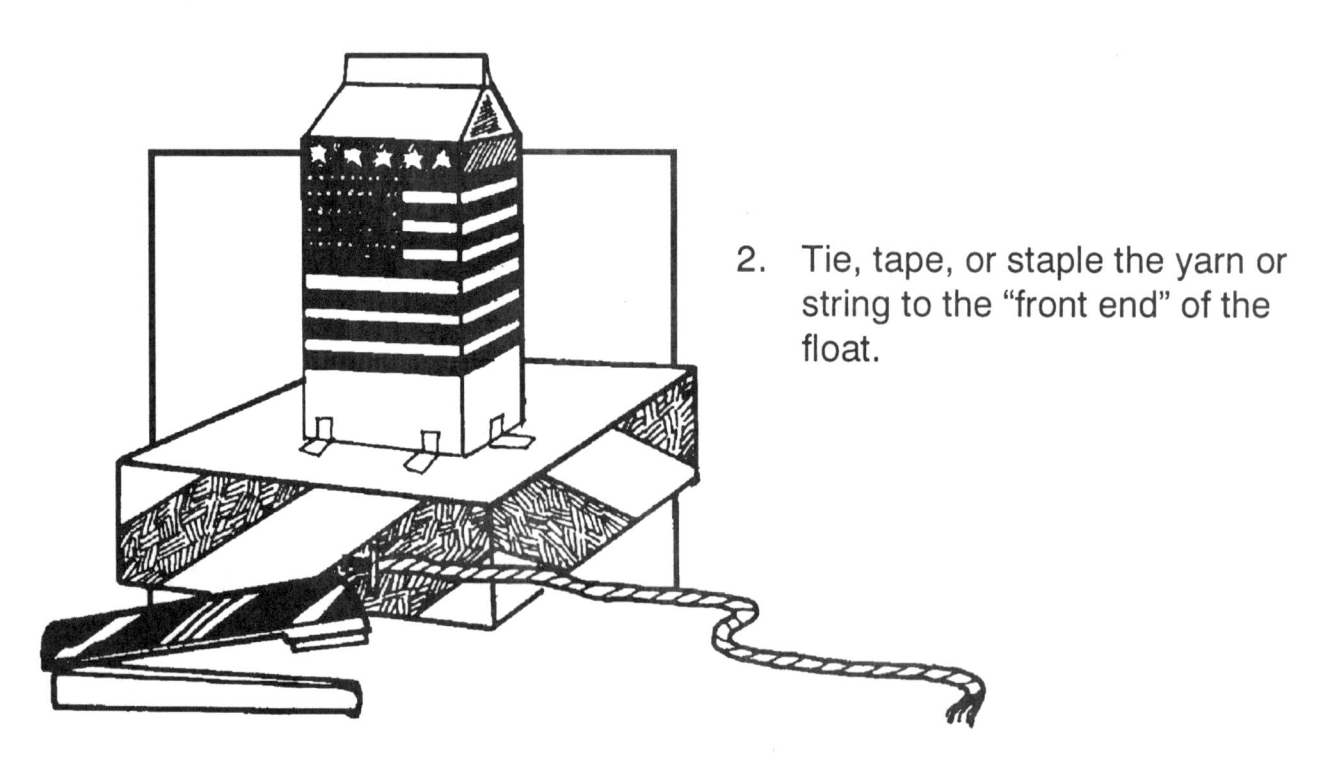

2. Tie, tape, or staple the yarn or string to the "front end" of the float.

#113 Hooray for the USA!

© 1991 Teacher Created Materials, Inc.

New Year's Day

Let's Have a Parade! *(cont.)*

3. Put a straw through the hole in the thread spool. Center the spool on the straw and fold both straw ends up evenly as shown.

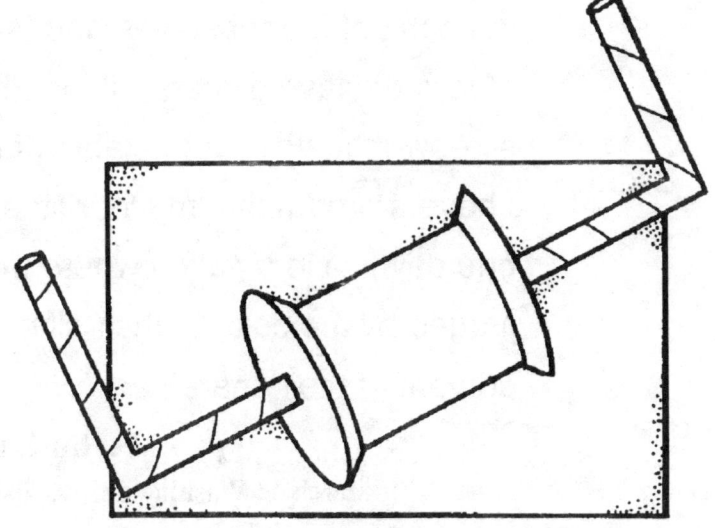

   Repeat the steps for the other straw and thread spool.

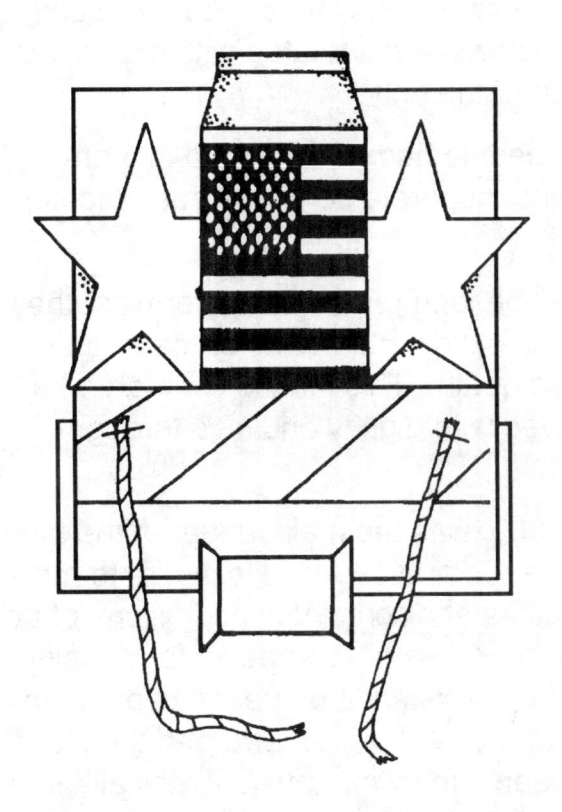

4. Securely attach the straw ends to the outside of the float with staples or tape.

You're ready to roll! Happy New Year!

When all floats are finished, they may be pulled by their creators across a floor or tabletop. To make the occasion more festive, add music, cheering, and popcorn!

© 1991 Teacher Created Materials, Inc.   23   #113 Hooray for the USA!

Martin Luther King, Jr.'s Birthday

> "I have a dream that one day . . .
>
> the sons of former slaves and the sons
>
> of former slave owners will be able to
>
> sit down together at the table of brotherhood . . .
>
> I have a dream that my four little children will
>
> one day live in a nation where they will not be
>
> judged by the color of their skin but by the
>
> content of their character."
>
> **Martin Luther King, Jr.**
> March on Washington, August 28, 1963

In the time of Abraham Lincoln and the Civil War, the Emancipation Proclamation of 1863 guaranteed freedom to the many slaves held captive in the United States. But in some states, Blacks were not allowed to be free. They were still treated with disrespect and inequality. For many, this new freedom was in name only.

Nearly 100 years later, the plight of the Black people had not changed in many states. There were separate schools, separate housing, separate service areas, and separate drinking fountains—separate and not equal.

Many Blacks fought for equality, and many will be long remembered for what they did. One of these courageous people remains in the minds and hearts of the American people, and people throughout the world, long after his death. This man is Dr. Martin Luther King, Jr., and his message that goals can be achieved with dignity and love through nonviolence is still alive!

Martin Luther King, Jr., born on January 15, 1929, was the main leader of the movement for civil rights in the United States during the 1950s and 1960s. He spoke to many, many people about equality for Blacks and other victims of discrimination. Millions of people believed in the words King said and wrote. Throughout his campaign for equality, he urged a nonviolent approach, and because of his insistence on peaceful demonstrations, he was respected and followed by people of all races. He was awarded the Nobel Peace Prize in 1964, and earned the admiration of people the world over. Tragically, King was killed by an assassin's bullet on April 4, 1968. The world mourned this peaceful leader.

Each year, on the third Monday in January, the people of the United States honor this man on the national holiday that bears his name. On this day, many reflect upon who Martin Luther King, Jr. was, what he fought for, how he waged his nonviolent battle, and what happened to the world because he had the courage to stand up for what he dreamed could be possible.

Martin Luther King, Jr.'s Birthday

Peacefully

Written below and on the following activity pages, you will find a story. In this story, there is a conflict between two people that needs to be resolved. The character of Martin Luther King, Jr. urges the kids to settle their problem peacefully. You will write the conclusion of the story.

One day after school...

"Hey, Matt! Do you want to ride to the park and play baseball?"

"Sure, Jimmy! I've got my glove in my backpack."

"Last one there has to eat a lemon!"

"Get ready for a sour mouth!"

"That's what you think!"

Martin Luther King, Jr.'s Birthday

Peacefully (cont.)

Here is a continuation of the story of conflict.

Suddenly...

WATCH OUT!

You did that on purpose.

No I didn't. It just fell, really.

You're lying. You just wanted to win.

#113 Hooray for the USA! 26 © 1991 Teacher Created Materials, Inc.

Martin Luther King, Jr.'s Birthday

Peacefully (cont.)

Here is a continuation of the story of conflict. Add some of your own ideas in the speech bubbles.

"Oh, yeah?"

"Yeah! Want to fight about it?"

"Boys, boys! Can't you work this out peacefully?"

"Talk to each other."

Martin Luther King, Jr.'s Birthday

Peacefully (cont.)

Write your own solution for this story of conflict.

The End

#113 Hooray for the USA! 28 © 1991 Teacher Created Materials, Inc.

Presidents' Day

Presidents' Day

We celebrate Presidents' Day on the third Monday in February each year. It is a day on which we remember the people who have served our nation as the Presidents of the United States.

Two presidents are especially remembered on this day: George Washington, born on February 22, 1732, and Abraham Lincoln, born on February 12, 1809. Although the two men came from different times and different backgrounds, they both believed strongly in the ideals of democracy, equality, and freedom.

George Washington is known in American history as the "Father of our Country." He "fathered" our country in several ways. As commander of the Continental Army, he helped win independence for America from Great Britain during the Revolutionary War. Another thing he did was to serve as president to the convention that wrote the Constitution of the United States. And, as we all know, George Washington was the first President of the United States. He was well-loved and respected throughout the new nation. One of his officers, Henry Lee, said of George Washington that he was, "First in war, first in peace, and first in the hearts of his countrymen."

Abraham Lincoln, our 16th President, was a remarkable man and great leader. He believed in the ideals of democracy on which the United States was established. In the time of the great conflict of the Civil War, he knew that the most important thing he could do would be to save the Union. The United States was the example of democracy in the world and could not fail. He spoke constantly and clearly about the need to preserve this democracy the people of the United States had worked so hard to establish and maintain. Lincoln's strong belief that the country would not be divided in half, but could come together as one, gave hope to a country who needed such a leader. Many people saw Lincoln as the man who saved the United States. They also saw a man whose humble beginnings proved that in a democracy, even a poor boy from a small farm could grow up to be President.

These two men will always be remembered for their inspirational lives and outstanding leadership as Presidents of the United States.

Presidents' Day

George Washington Mosaic

Make a mosaic-type picture of George Washington using the pattern on this page and mosaic materials such as seeds, rock pieces, yarn, tiny paper squares, and sand.

Presidents' Day

Abraham Lincoln Mosaic

Make a mosaic-type picture of Abraham Lincoln using the pattern on this page and mosaic materials such as seeds, rock pieces, yarn, tiny paper squares, and sand.

© 1991 Teacher Created Materials, Inc.   31   #113 Hooray for the USA!

Presidents' Day

Presidential Money Math

Presidents of the United States have been pictured on United States coins and paper money. Here is a review for you.

penny: Abraham Lincoln

16th President

nickel: Thomas Jefferson

3rd President

dime: Franklin D. Roosevelt

32nd President

quarter: George Washington

1st President

half-dollar: John F. Kennedy

35th President

Here are some familiar Presidents' faces found on paper money:

1 dollar bill: George Washington

1st President

5 dollar bill: Abraham Lincoln

16th President

20 dollar bill: Andrew Jackson

7th President

Use this review paper to help you on the following "Presidential Money Math" pages.

Presidents' Day

Presidential Money Math *(cont.)*

Count the money in each box. Write the total on the line.

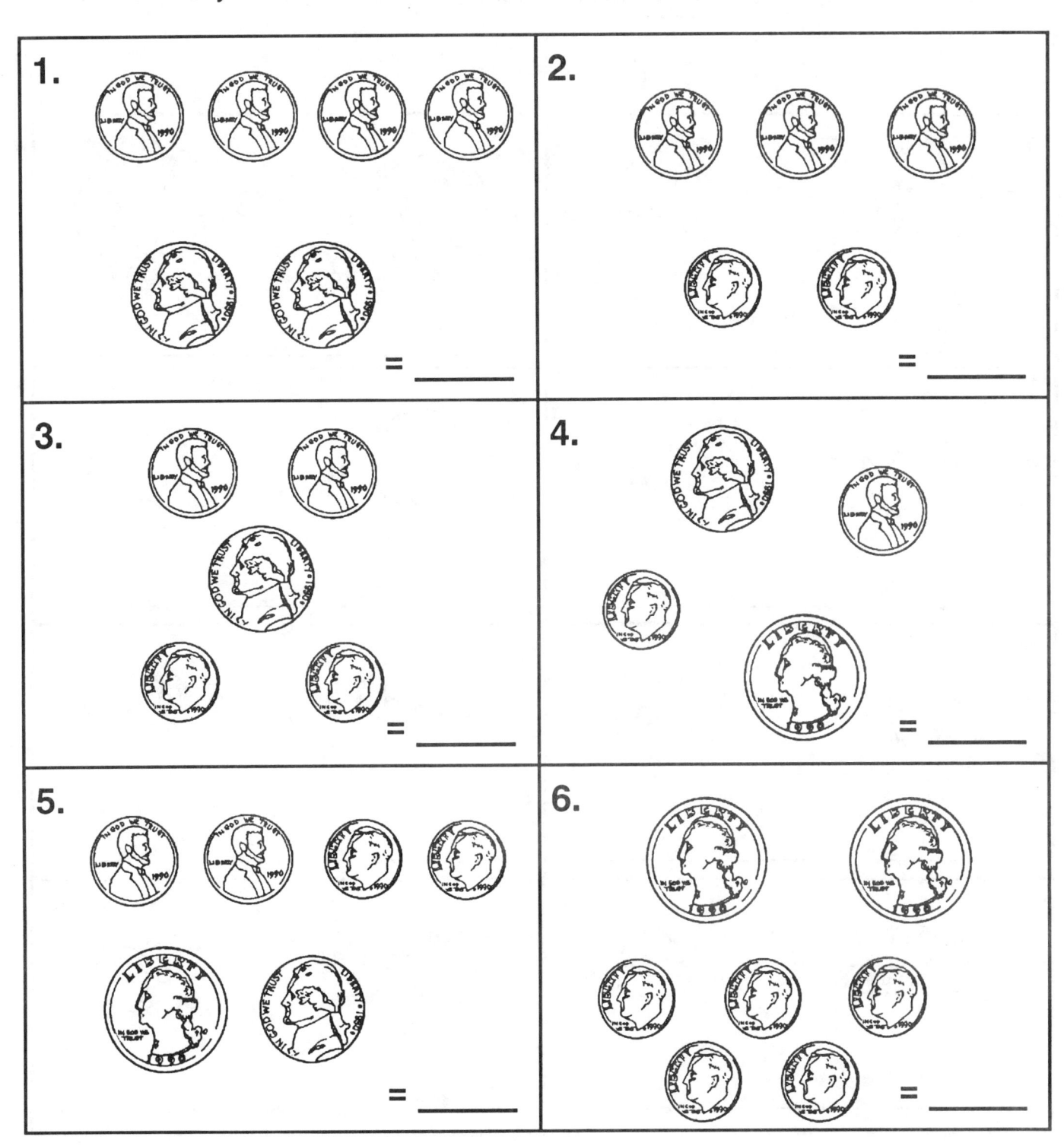

1. = _____

2. = _____

3. = _____

4. = _____

5. = _____

6. = _____

Answer Key (Cover before duplicating.)

1) 14¢ 2) 23¢ 3) 27¢ 4) 41¢ 5) 52¢ 6) $1.00

© 1991 Teacher Created Materials, Inc.   #113 Hooray for the USA!

Presidents' Day

Presidential Money Math (cont.)

Below each picture write the total value of the coins and paper money. Then write an =, <, or > between each.

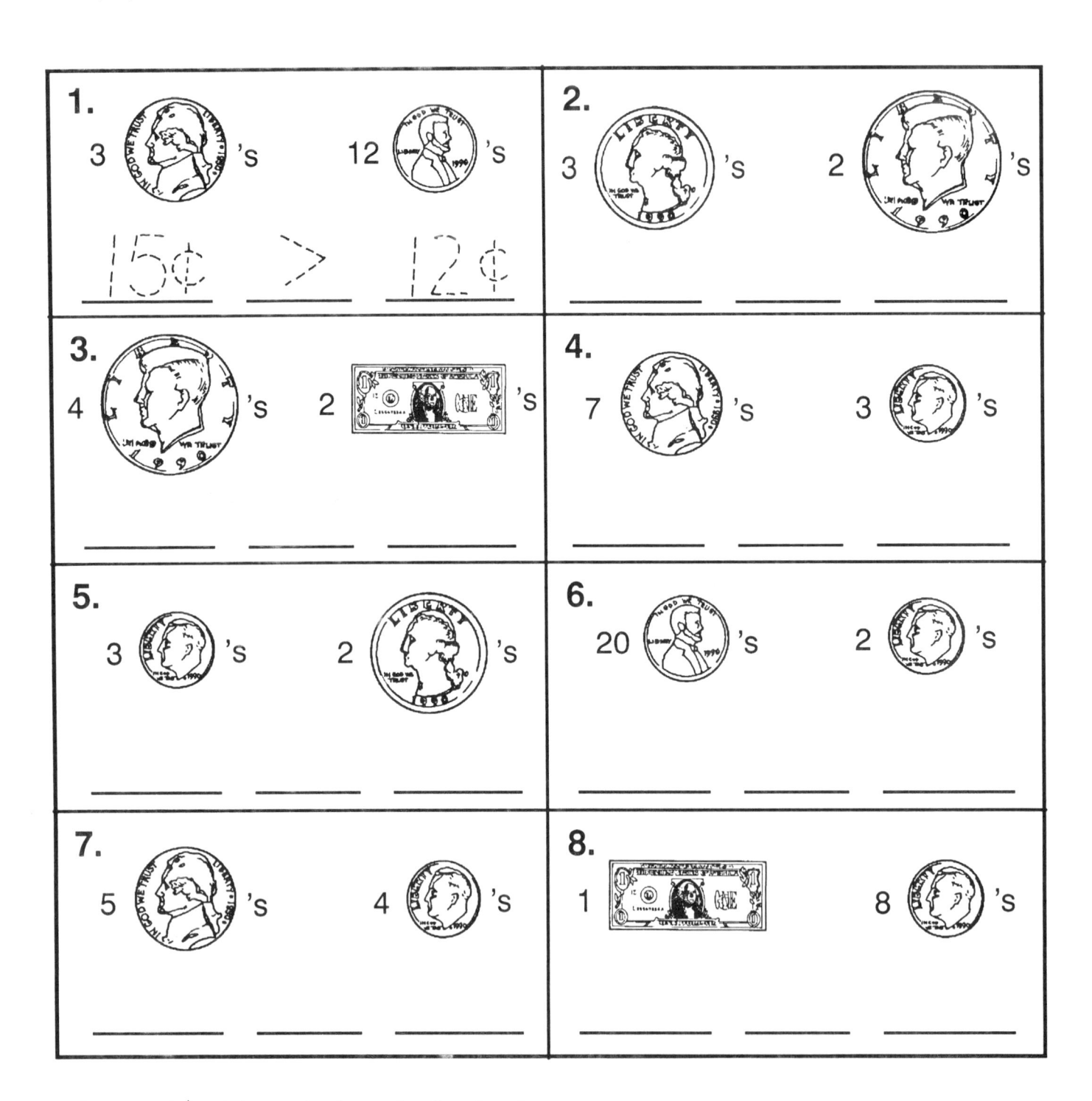

---

1. 3 (nickel)'s   12 (penny)'s

15¢ > 12¢

2. 3 (quarter)'s   2 (half dollar)'s

_____

3. 4 (half dollar)'s   2 ($1 bill)'s

_____

4. 7 (nickel)'s   3 (dime)'s

_____

5. 3 (dime)'s   2 (quarter)'s

_____

6. 20 (penny)'s   2 (dime)'s

_____

7. 5 (nickel)'s   4 (dime)'s

_____

8. 1 ($1 bill)'s   8 (dime)'s

_____

Answer key (Cover before duplicating.)

1) 15¢ > 12¢   2) 75¢ < $1.00   3) $2.00 = $2.00   4) 35¢ > 30¢

5) 30¢ < 50¢   6) 20¢ = 20¢   7) 25¢ < 40¢   8) $1.00 > 80¢

#113 Hooray for the USA!   34   © 1991 Teacher Created Materials, Inc.

Presidents' Day

Presidential Money Math

Complete the following "Presidential Money Math" quiz.

1. _____ How many Lincoln pennies equal a Kennedy half-dollar?
2. _____ How many Jefferson nickels equal a Kennedy half-dollar?
3. _____ How many Roosevelt dimes equal a Kennedy half-dollar?
4. _____ How many Washington quarters equal a Kennedy half-dollar?
5. _____ Lincoln, Jefferson, Roosevelt, and Washington coins can all be used to equal a Kennedy half-dollar.

   Write the possible combinations on the lines below.

   _____ = 50 cents
   _____ = 50 cents

6. _____ How many Washington coins are needed to equal a Washington bill?
7. _____ How many Lincoln coins are needed to equal a Lincoln bill?
8. _____ How many Kennedy coins are needed to equal a Lincoln bill?
9. _____ How many Roosevelt coins are needed to equal a Washington bill?
10. _____ How many Lincoln bills are needed to equal a Jackson bill?

Make some "Presidential Money Math" quiz questions of your own!

Answer Key (Cover before duplicating.)

1) 50   2) 10   3) 5   4) 2   5) 1 q + 1 d + 2 n + 5 p; 1 q + 1 d + 1 n + 10 p
6) 4   7) 500   8) 10   9) 10   10) 4

© 1991 Teacher Created Materials, Inc.   35   #113 Hooray for the USA!

Arbor Day

Arbor Day

The planting of trees has been celebrated for hundreds and hundreds of years all over the world. People know just how important trees are to the survival of Earth.

The first Arbor Day in the United States was the idea of Julius Sterling Morton. He wanted to help change the barren way his state of Nebraska looked. It was almost treeless because the people who had settled on the Nebraska plains had chopped down most of the trees for firewood and home building. Morton knew that trees helped to nourish the land and hold moisture in it. He was responsible for the first Arbor Day being celebrated on April 10, 1872. Later, when he died, the people of Nebraska changed Arbor Day to Mr. Morton's birthday, April 22, and made it a legal holiday.

As the popularity of Arbor Day grew, other states began to celebrate it as well. Now, most of the provinces in Canada and states in the United States celebrate this special time of tree planting. Californians celebrate Arbor Day on March 7, the birthdate of Luther Burbank, a famous plant specialist. Hawaii and many of the southern states have Arbor Day dates that range from December to March. Most northern states celebrate the day in April or May, when spring has thawed the ground.

Countries throughout the world have celebrations for the honoring of trees. They are often called Tree Holiday or Tree Festival. In Japan, it is called Greening Week. In Iceland, it is called Student Afforestation Day. Tree Loving Week takes place in Korea, and Israel has a New Year's Day of the Trees. In India, they call their celebration the National Festival of Tree Planting. In Yugoslavia, the spring holiday is Arbor Day, while the fall holiday is called Afforestation Day.

Arbor Day is a special day when people who love trees, plant and celebrate them! Work together to plan an Arbor Day celebration in your school or community, complete with songs, poems, tree-planting, and dedication ceremony. Show your love for trees!

"Other holidays repose upon the past,

Arbor Day proposes for the future."

-Julius Sterling Morton

Arbor Day

Arbor Day Coloring Book

Make an "Arbor Day Coloring Book." Some pages are started for you, but be sure to add a lot more of your own ideas and drawings to the book!

Trees make the world more beautiful.

Arbor Day

Arbor Day Coloring Book *(cont.)*

You might want to use some of these ideas for pages in your coloring book: Trees give us shade, food, and oxygen to breathe. Trees help to lessen noise and air pollution. Trees also give us many things we use everyday, such as wood, paper, and pencils.

Trees are homes for all kinds of animals.

Arbor Day

Arbor Day Coloring Book *(cont.)*

You might want to use some of these ideas for pages in your coloring book: Trees help keep the soil from washing away and trees hold moisture in the ground. Trees help to enrich the soil with their old leaves and branches. They also smell good!

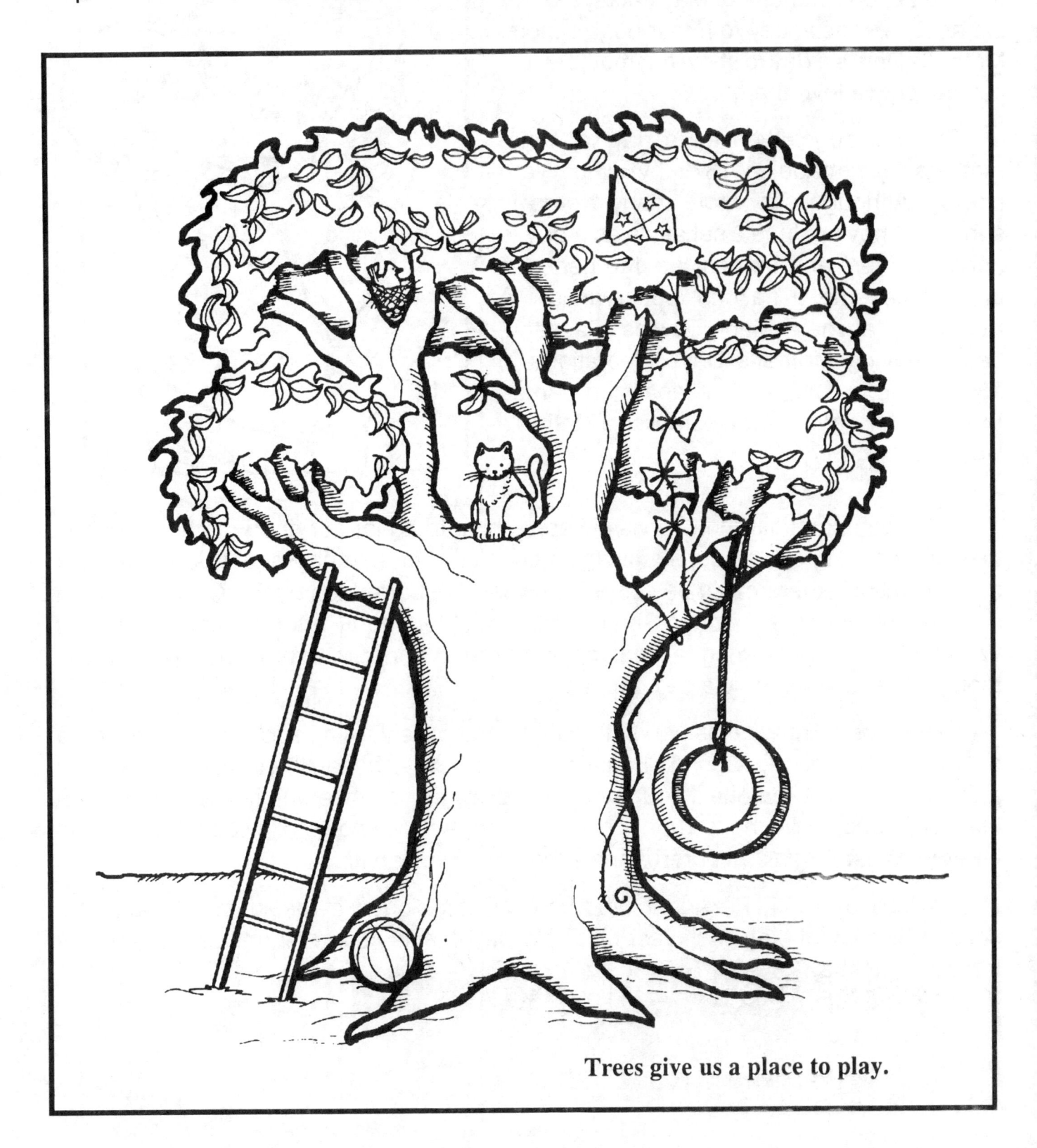

Trees give us a place to play.

© 1991 Teacher Created Materials, Inc.   39   #113 Hooray for the USA!

Mother's Day and Father's Day

Mother's Day

The second Sunday of May each year, we set aside a special day to honor our mothers. Mother's Day is a day to show our mothers just how much we love them.

The first suggestion for a day to honor mothers was made in 1872 by Julia Ward Howe. Although she wrote many words in support of having June 2 set aside as a day to honor mothers and be dedicated to peace, it did not become a national observance. A Kentucky teacher, Mary Towles Sasseen, began having Mother's Day celebrations in 1887. And in 1904, an Indiana man named Frank E. Hering worked to establish a Mother's Day in our country.

But it was not until Anna Jarvis did something to honor her dead mother's wishes that Mother's Day gained popularity and recognition. Mrs. Anna Reeves Jarvis, Anna's mother, wished there could be some way when the hatred fed by the Civil War could be forgotten, if only for a day. She told her daughter shortly after the end of the Civil War, that the once warring factions could agree to honor their mothers. Mrs. Jarvis thought this day could be a day of peace.

Years later, Anna Jarvis began to campaign actively for a nationwide observance of Mother's Day on the second Sunday of May. She also began the tradition of wearing a carnation, a colored one if your mother is alive, and a white one if she is dead. On May 10, 1908, a Mother's Day service at Andrews Methodist Episcopal Church in Grafton, West Virginia honored Anna's mother, Mrs. Jarvis.

On May 9, 1914, President Woodrow Wilson signed a resolution to make the second Sunday of May each year Mother's Day in every state. It has become a very treasured holiday.

Mother's Day and Father's Day

Father's Day

The third Sunday of June each year we set aside as a special day to honor our fathers. Father's Day is a day to show our fathers just how much we love them.

The idea for a Mother's Day in the United States started in 1872 but did not become "official" until 1914. But how about Father's Day?

Sonora Louise Smart Dodd, along with her brothers and sisters, was raised lovingly by her father after the death of her mother. Her father was very dear to her. She decided a special day should be set aside each year to honor fathers, just as mothers had received honor. She worked toward this end, and on June 19, 1910, her hometown of Spokane, Washington celebrated the first Father's Day.

But it took many years before Father's Day was recognized as a national holiday. In 1936, a national Father's Day Committee was formed to campaign for the holiday. But it wasn't until 1972, over 60 years since that first Spokane Father's Day celebration, that President Richard M. Nixon made the national holiday law. This holiday, like Mother's Day, has become a very treasured occasion.

Mother's Day and Father's Day

Mother's Day and Father's Day Projects

Many early cards were made with dried flowers, shells, fabric, pieces of ribbon and lace, and other materials that look pretty. Often, the cards were left blank in the inside so the sender could write a message.

Make an old-fashioned Mother's or Father's Day card. Here are some types of materials and designs you can use.

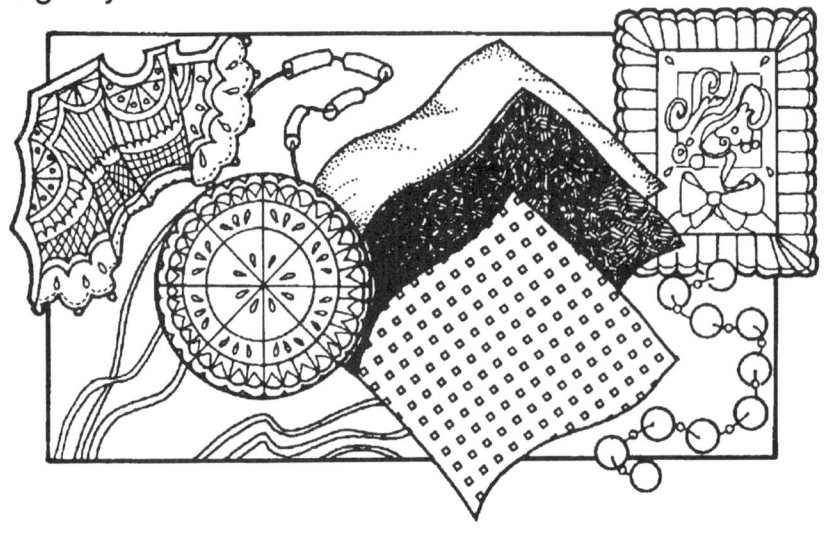

You might want to make a different type of card for your mother or father, such as a pop-up. Here are some ideas.

Whatever kind of card you make, write some words inside the card that show how you feel about your mother or father. Make it as special as you can!

Mother's Day and Father's Day

Mother's Day and Father's Day Projects *(cont.)*

Here is an idea for a poem that you can do.

ACROSTIC GREETING

Write "Mother" or "Father" vertically on a blank sheet of paper.

M F
O A
T T   or
H H
E E
R R

Think of things that your mother and father do that make you like them so much.

You must use the first letter of each name to start your words or phrases.

M akes my days special by going for walks with me

O ffers me help when I'm having trouble doing things

T akes time to listen to me

H as a van and takes my friends places with me

E ats ice cream exactly the way I do

R eally loves me

F antastic

A rtistic

T ender

H appy

E ver-loving

R ad!

Make one or more of these greetings for your parents!

Mother's Day and Father's Day

Mother's Day and Father's Day Projects (cont.)

Make coupons to give to your mother and father. On each coupon, write one thing you will do for them. Here are some ideas. You probably can think of many of your own ideas, too!

I will clean my room without being asked for one week.
I will come the first time I am called for one day.
I will make you breakfast this Sunday.
I will rake the leaves before dinner.
I will give you 10 hugs sometime today.
I will not tease my brother or sister for three days.
I will do my house jobs cheerfully today.
I will draw you a special picture.

Here are some coupons you can use. Fill them in with things you know will make your mother and father happy! Color them, cut them out, and give them to your parents.

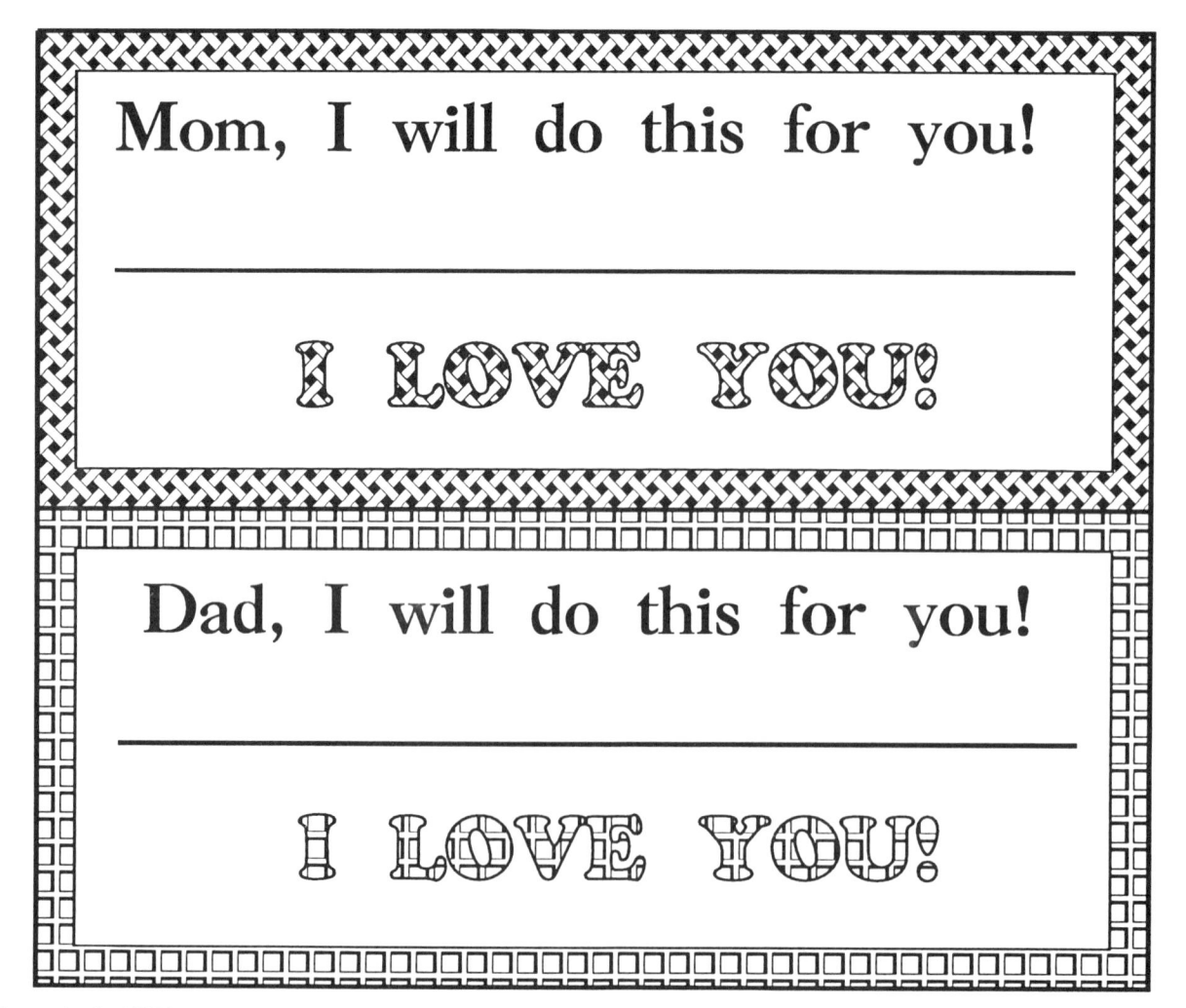

Mom, I will do this for you!
_____
I LOVE YOU!

Dad, I will do this for you!
_____
I LOVE YOU!

Mother's Day and Father's Day

Mother's Day and Father's Day Projects *(cont.)*

Draw a picture of yourself to give to your mother or father for Mother's Day or Father's Day. Decorate the frame on this page. Cut out the inside section of the frame, and place your picture behind it, attaching your picture to the frame with tape. Cut a piece of colored tagboard to match the size of the frame and glue the edges of the frame and tagboard together.

Give yourself to your parents!

cut out

Memorial Day

Memorial Day

Memorial Day is an American patriotic holiday when we honor those who gave their lives in the service of their country. It is a time for us to think about those people whose lives have been lost and thoughtfully remember them.

The idea of a day for remembering those who have died for our country began in the time after the Civil War. Henry C. Welles, a resident of Waterloo, New York, decided that something should be done to honor those soldiers who died in the Civil War. It was a time when nearly all families suffered the loss of loved ones. It was a time when the states of the United States were torn apart, when brother fought brother, father fought son, and cousin fought cousin. Welles believed that respect could be shown for the dead by decorating their graves with flowers and flags. Those who fought in the war and survived could also be honored by a parade on the way to the grave decoration ceremony at the cemetery. On May 5, 1866, the first Decoration Day was held.

Near the same time, General John A. Logan commanded a large group of veterans from the North called the Grand Army of the Republic. They decorated the graves of Union soldiers on May 30. In 1868, the two decoration days were celebrated together on May 30. Many of the Southern states had (and continue to have) days for honoring the Confederate dead.

The name for the day of remembering was changed from Decoration Day to Memorial Day in 1882. In 1971, Memorial Day became a national holiday. It is celebrated on the last Monday in May with parades and memorial services. It is a day set aside for remembering all who have died in the service of the United States in times of war.

Memorial Day

Memorial Day Bouquet

Make flowers according to these directions. Arrange the finished flowers in a bouquet. Use the bouquets for a Memorial Day celebration or present them to a group such as the American Legion. Members of this or a similar group can help you and your classmates distribute the bouquets appropriately.

Here are some ideas for making your flowers.

TRIPLE TISSUE FLOWERS

To make each flower you will need:

* 1 yellow pipe cleaner

* 3 pieces of tissue paper (You may choose three different shades of the same color or three different colors.)

* florist tape

Directions

1. Cut tissue according to the patterns and directions on page 48. Be sure to make your largest circle the darkest tissue color and your smallest circle the lightest.

2. Stack all three circles together, with the darkest color on the bottom and the lightest on top.

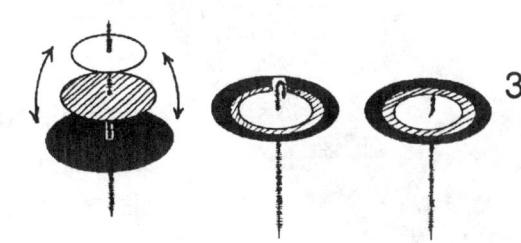

3. Push the end of a yellow pipe cleaner up through the stacked colors until it sticks up through the papers about 1 to 1 1/2 inches (2.5 to 4 centimeters).

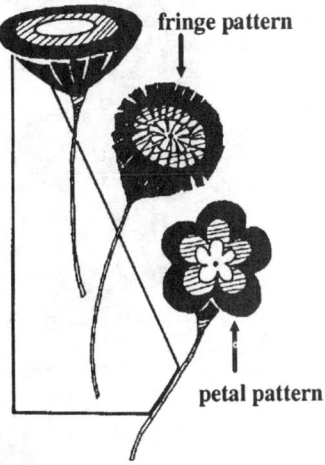

4. Bend the top of the pipe cleaner in half and pinch the bent part together to form the flower's stamen.

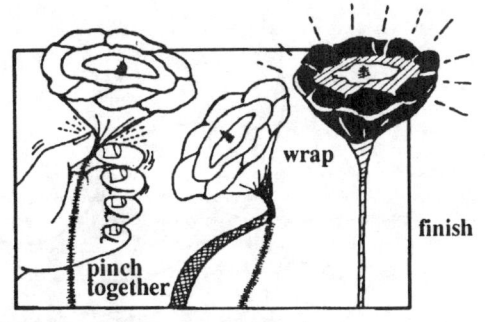

5. Pinch the bottom of the flower petals until the flower is the shape that you like. Then tightly wrap the florist tape around the bottom of the petals. Continue wrapping the tape in a downward motion until you reach the end of the pipe cleaner.

© 1991 Teacher Created Materials, Inc.   47   #113 Hooray for the USA!

Memorial Day

Memorial Day Bouquet

Make flowers according to these directions. Use them to make a Memorial Day bouquet.

Use these pattern sizes and shape ideas for making your Triple Tissue Flowers.

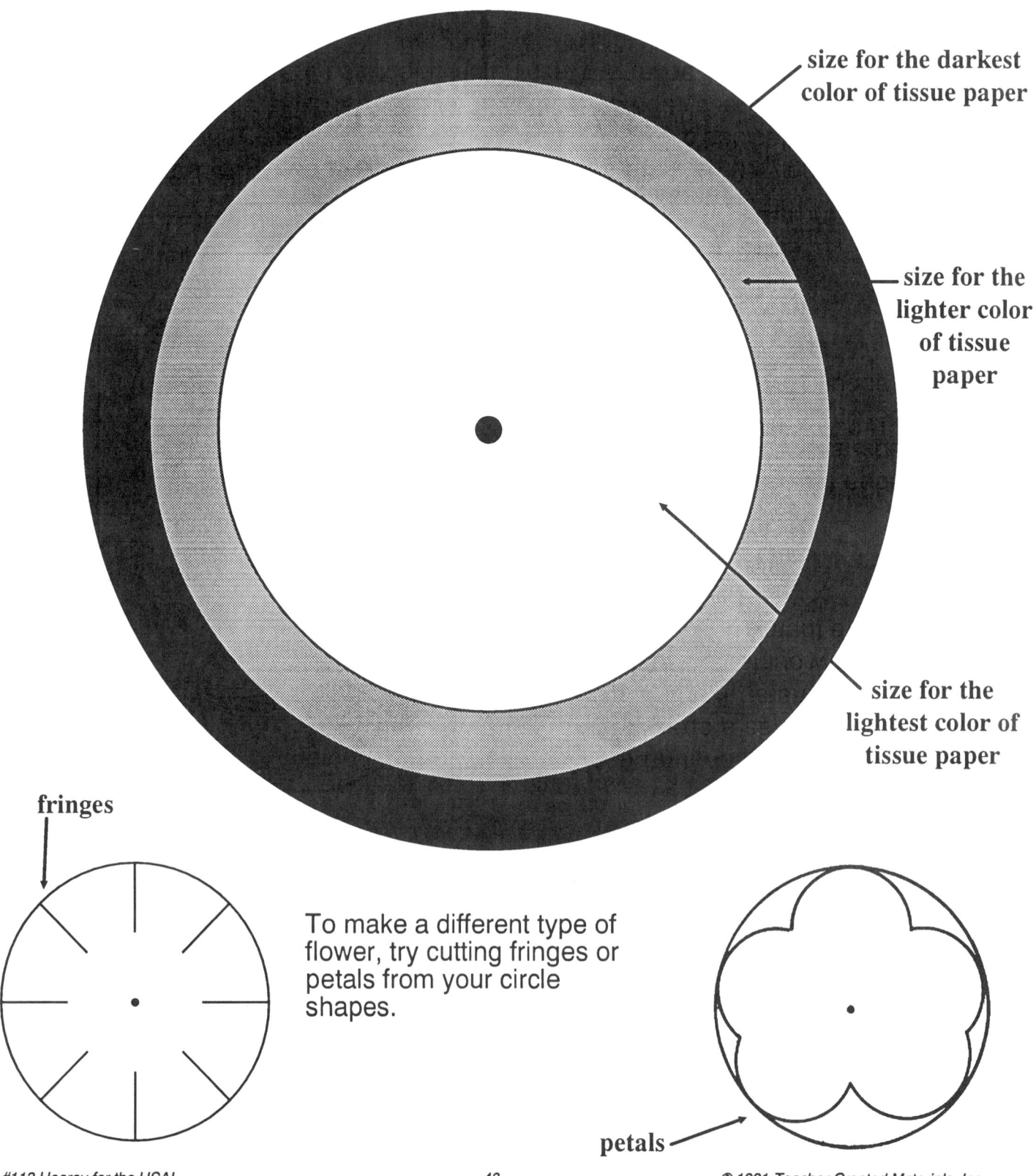

size for the darkest color of tissue paper

size for the lighter color of tissue paper

size for the lightest color of tissue paper

fringes

To make a different type of flower, try cutting fringes or petals from your circle shapes.

petals

#113 Hooray for the USA! © 1991 Teacher Created Materials, Inc.

Memorial Day

Memorial Day Bouquet

Here is another type of flower you can make.

TISSUE FLOWERS

To make each flower you will need:

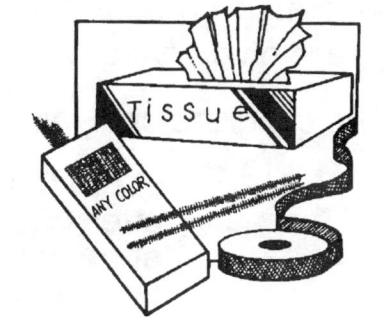

* 1 piece of facial tissue per flower (Use any color you would like.)
* 1 pipe cleaner (Use any color.)
* florist tape

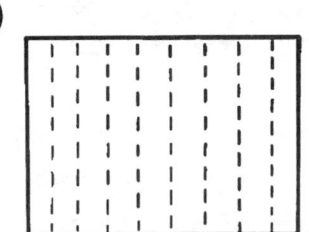

Directions

1. Flatten tissue on a flat surface.
2. Fold tissue like a fan on lines as shown. Fold, then flip tissue over. Fold, flip over again, until all of the tissue is folded.

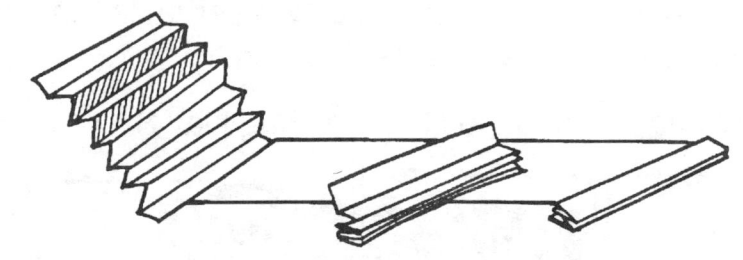

3. Hold the folded tissue in one hand and cut the ends into one of these shapes:

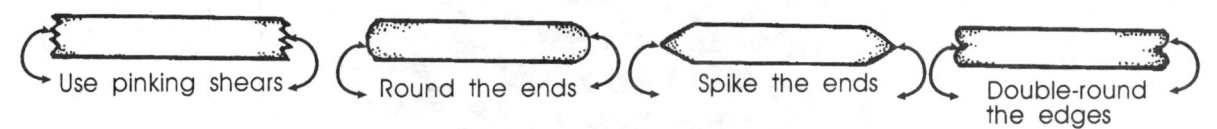

    Use pinking shears — Round the ends — Spike the ends — Double-round the edges

4. Pinch the folded tissue in the middle. Then hold the pinched tissue in place by fastening it with the end of the pipe cleaner.

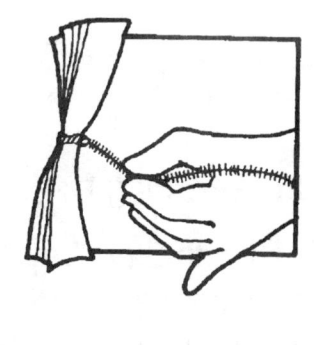

5. Carefully pull the tissue petals toward the center and fluff gently.

6. Pinch the bottom of the petals together firmly. Wrap with florist tape until the entire pipe cleaner is covered with tape.

Enjoy your flowers!

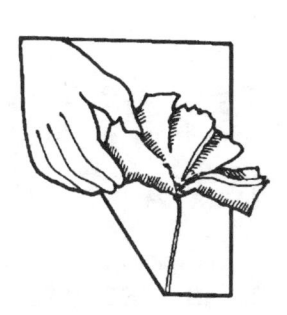

Flag Day

Flag Day

While Flag Day is not an official national holiday, it is a day that is recognized by the President of the United States each year as the day to honor our flag. Flag Day is celebrated on June 14 to commemorate the day in 1777 when the Continental Congress officially adopted the flag of stars and stripes as the symbol of our country.

The congressional resolution stated:

> **"That the flag of the United States be 13 stripes, alternately red and white, and that the Union be 13 stars, white in a blue field, representing a new constellation."**

The first Flag Day celebration was on June 14, 1877, the 100th anniversary of the adoption of the flag. Each year after, special ceremonies marked this day. In 1916, President Woodrow Wilson proclaimed June 14 as Flag Day. Later, during the time of World War I, President Wilson remarked in one of his speeches,

"This flag, which we honor, and under which we serve, is the emblem of our unity, our power, our thought, and our purpose as a nation."

President Harry Truman signed the National Flag Day Bill in 1949, officially making June 14 Flag Day.

Each Flag Day, people all over the United States show their feelings for the flag of their country by displaying it proudly. Many schools and organizations hold special ceremonies to honor the flag and discuss its history. Often, there are Flag Day parades.

Flag Day is a day that is special to all who cherish the flag.

#113 Hooray for the USA! 50 © 1991 Teacher Created Materials, Inc.

Flag Day

Honoring Our Flag

The flag of the United States is a symbol to be treated with respect.

Here are some rules for displaying the flag with honor. Cut out each of these boxes that hold the rules. Paste or glue them under the appropriate pictures on the following activity pages.

Do not display the flag if the weather could damage it.	Display the flag from sunrise to sunset.
Do not hang the flag upside down. That signals a serious emergency.	The flag of the United States may not be used for clothing. Use the colors, not the flag.
If the flag is flown at night, use a spotlight to make it show.	Do not let the flag touch the ground.
Carefully fold the flag when it is not being displayed.	When carried, the flag should be able to wave freely.

© 1991 Teacher Created Materials, Inc.   51   #113 Hooray for the USA!

Flag Day

Honoring Our Flag (cont.)

Color the pictures below. Then paste or glue in the appropriate rules.

#113 Hooray for the USA! © 1991 Teacher Created Materials, Inc.

Flag Day

Honoring Our Flag (cont.)

Color the pictures below. Then paste or glue in the appropriate rules.

© 1991 Teacher Created Materials, Inc.   #113 Hooray for the USA!

Independence Day

Independence Day

On Independence Day, the Fourth of July, the people of the United States celebrate the anniversary of the founding of our democratic nation. The signs of the holiday are all around. Flags are unfurled around the countryside, people cover the parks and recreation areas with picnics, Uncle Sam leads town parades, patriotic music fills the air, and spectacular fireworks light up the sky! It is a noisy, joyous day!

Independence Day is the birthday of the United States. On July 4, 1776, over 200 years ago, the United Colonies of America adopted the document which declared the United States to be "Free and Independent States," and that "all political connection between them and the State of Great Britain, is and ought to be totally dissolved." This document was the Declaration of Independence which gave all who lived in these new United States the equal right to "Life, Liberty, and the Pursuit of Happiness."

The Declaration of Independence set up the foundation for freedom and democracy in our country and inspired many people throughout the world to be free.

The first Independence Day celebration took place in Philadelphia on July 4, 1777. It was a grand day of celebration. Through the years, the Fourth of July has been kept as a special holiday by the people of the United States. It's a day filled with historic remembering, a rededication to democracy, and a whole lot of fun!

Independence Day

The Celebration!

Plan an Independence Day celebration for your family, your neighborhood, or your community.

Here are some ideas to help you get started.

* Hold a planning meeting. See how many people would be interested in helping to plan a Fourth of July celebration. Decide on the types of things you would like to see included in your day of celebration.

* Make a list of the events of the day. Some events might be as follows:

a parade	a patriotic song sing-along
a fun run	a presentation of historical moments from 1776
a picnic	readings of patriotic speeches and poems
picnic games	a family, neighborhood, or community cook-out
contests	a safe fireworks display

* Assign jobs to different responsible people.

* Arrange for music. (The words for three patriotic songs are written on pages 57-59.)

* Publicize the event in a flyer or community newspaper.

* Make a program for the event. (A sample program is included on page 56.)

* Meet with your co-workers to iron out any last minute details.

* Enjoy your celebration! You should feel good that you helped make this special day more special!

© 1991 Teacher Created Materials, Inc. #113 Hooray for the USA!

Independence Day

The Celebration! (cont.)

Here is a sample program design that you may use.

Independence Day Program

Come celebrate!

9:00   Patriotic Speeches
9:30   Patriotic Sing-Along
10:00   Games
      *Wheelbarrow Games
      *Horseshoes
      *Softball

12:00   Picnic Cook-out
2:00   Parade

After Dark—Fireworks Display!

#113 Hooray for the USA!   © 1991 Teacher Created Materials, Inc.

Independence Day

The Celebration! (cont.)

People who love their country enjoy singing patriotic songs. We have many patriotic songs in the United States. You may already know some of them. But, as you sing the ones you know or listen to others, do you really stop to think about what the words mean?

Read the words of the patriotic songs found on the next few pages. Think about what each song means. Discuss the words and their meaning with others. You may even want to sing these songs and discuss their meanings during your day of celebration!

AMERICA THE BEAUTIFUL

by Katherine Lee Bates

O beautiful for spacious skies,
For amber waves of grain,
For purple mountain majesties
Above the fruited plain!
America! America!
God shed His grace on thee
And crown thy good with brotherhood
From sea to shining sea!

O beautiful for pilgrim feet,
Whose stern, impassioned stress
A thoroughfare for freedom beat
Across the wilderness!
America! America!
God mend thine every flaw,
Confirm thy soul in self-control,
Thy liberty in law!

O beautiful for heroes proved
In liberating strife,
Who more than self their country loved,
And mercy more than life!
America! America!
May God thy gold refine
Till all success be nobleness,
And every gain divine!

O beautiful for patriot dream
That sees beyond the years
Thine alabaster cities gleam
Undimmed by human tears!
America! America!
God shed His grace on thee
And crown thy good with brotherhood
From sea to shining sea!

Independence Day

The Celebration! (cont.)

Read and discuss these words to one of the United States' popular patriotic songs.

AMERICA
by Samuel Francis Smith

My country, 'tis of thee,
Sweet land of liberty,
　Of thee I sing;
Land where my fathers died,
Land of the pilgrims' pride,
From every mountain-side
　Let freedom ring.

My native country, thee,
Land of the noble free,
　Thy name I love;
I love thy rocks and rills,
Thy woods and templed hills;
My heart with rapture thrills
　Like that above.

Let music swell the breeze,
And ring from all the trees
　Sweet freedom's song;
Let mortal tongues awake,
Let all that breathe partake,
Let rocks their silence break
　The sound prolong.

Our fathers' God, to Thee,
Author of liberty,
　To Thee we sing;
Long may our land be bright
With freedom's holy light;
Protect us by Thy might,
　Great God, our King.

Independence Day

The Celebration! (cont.)

Read and discuss these words of the National Anthem.

THE STAR-SPANGLED BANNER
by Francis Scott Key

O say! can you see, by the dawn's early light,
What so proudly we hail'd at the twilight's last gleaming?
Whose broad stripes and bright stars, thro' the perilous fight,
O'er the ramparts we watch'd, were so gallantly streaming?
And the rocket's red glare, the bombs bursting in air,
Gave proof thro' the night that our flag was still there.
O say, does that Star-spangled Banner yet wave
O'er the land of the free and the home of the brave!

On the shore, dimly seen thro' the mists of the deep,
Where the foe's haughty host in dread silence reposes,
What is that which the breeze, o'er the towering steep,
As it fitfully blows, half conceals, half discloses?
Now it catches the gleam of the morning's first beam,
In full glory reflected now shines on the stream;
'Tis the Star-spangled Banner, O long may it wave
O'er the land of the free and the home of the brave!

O thus be it ever when freemen shall stand
Between their loved homes and the war's desolation!
Blest with vict'ry and peace, may the heav'n rescued land
Praise the Pow'r that hath made and preserved us a nation!
Then conquer we must, when our cause it is just,
And this be our motto; "In God is our trust!"
And the Star-spangled Banner in triumph shall wave
O'er the land of the free and the home of the brave!

Labor Day

Labor Day

To labor means to work. Labor Day is a national holiday that honors all people who work by giving them a day off work to rest and "play." It is celebrated on the first Monday of September. But there was not always a Labor Day. The idea for a Labor Day began over 100 years ago in New York City.

The people in New York City and other places throughout the country wanted to work. They took pride in what they did. But the conditions they worked under were not the best. They often worked long hours, sometimes 12 to 14 hours a day, six or seven days a week. Laborers were underpaid and worked in places that were not safe. By the time children were 11 or 12, they often had to work to help support the family, and their workday was usually 10 hours.

The unhappy workers joined together to form unions, which united people in the same trades. These unions were able to speak in a louder voice to make their needs known. Some of the smaller unions joined together to form a Central Labor Union. These union members fought to get better working conditions. And along with improved conditions for work, they also wanted a special holiday to honor all laborers.

The first Labor Day was organized by the New York Central Labor Union and scheduled to be on Monday, September 5, 1882. It was a huge success. Over 10,000 workers marched in the parade and over 50,000 people filled Elm Park for a day of picnics, speeches, music, and family fun. The day ended with fireworks.

Workers throughout America liked this idea of Labor Day. The next year, hundreds of cities held Labor Day celebrations. And in 1894, Labor Day became a national holiday.

We continue to celebrate Labor Day in the tradition of those workers of long ago. We have a day off work and school, sharing food and fun with our families and friends.

#113 Hooray for the USA!   © 1991 Teacher Created Materials, Inc.

Labor Day

Job Book Cover

You will be working in your class to make a "Job Book." You can make your job book as long as you'd like. On the following pages are some ideas you can use.

Job Book

by

_____

© 1991 Teacher Created Materials, Inc.   61   #113 Hooray for the USA!

Labor Day

Job Graph

Make a chart of the types of jobs held by the parents of students in your classroom. Make as many copies of this chart as needed to represent the diversity of jobs held by the parents. List the jobs on the left side of the chart.

THE JOBS OF OUR PARENTS		
Type of Job for Parent	Names of Students	Total

#113 Hooray for the USA! © 1991 Teacher Created Materials, Inc.

Labor Day

Interview Sheet

Invite parents to speak to the class about the careers they have chosen. Prepare for each speaker by learning something about the job before the parent comes in to speak. Be ready to interview the parents after they talk about their jobs.

Let's Find Out About...

_____
(type of job)

What I have discovered about this job before hearing the speakers:

_____
_____

Date of Parent Presentation: _____
Parent to make Presentation: _____
Parent of: _____
What I learned from this parent's presentation:

_____
_____
_____

Some questions to ask the parent about his or her job:
1. Do you like what you do? _____ Why? _____
_____
2. How long have you had this job? _____
3. What kind of training does this job take? _____
4. Do you think you will always want to do this job? _____
5. Would you like your son or daughter to have this job, too? Please explain.
_____
_____

Labor Day

In the Past and Now

Some of the jobs that people had 100 years ago are the same as jobs people have today. People still are bricklayers, printers, carpenters, miners, factory workers, and machinists. Make a chart that shows how these jobs have changed in 100 years.

JOBS IN THE PAST COMPARED WITH THE SAME JOBS TODAY	
100 Years Ago	Today
BRICKLAYERS *(Think about how bricks are made, carried, and used.)*	
PRINTERS *(Think about modern machinery, ways information is collected, and how news can be learned.)*	
CARPENTERS *(Think about how tools, materials, and people's needs have changed.)*	

#113 Hooray for the USA! © 1991 Teacher Created Materials, Inc.

Labor Day

Your Job!

What kind of job would you like to have in the future? What kind of training will you have to have for this job? Do you think you will be able to get this kind of job? Is it the kind of job that will make you happy? Complete this job description form.

My Job!

My name: _____

The job I want to have in the future: _____
_____

Job Description:
_____
_____

Training I will have to have:
_____
_____

Salary: _____

Why I think I would be good at this job:
_____
_____

Good points about this job:
_____
_____

Bad points about this job:
_____
_____

Other kids I know who might like this job:
_____
_____

The United States Flag

One of the most loved symbols of our country is the American flag. It stands for many things.

The thirteen stripes in our flag, seven red and six white, stand for the thirteen colonies that joined together in 1776 to declare themselves free from the rule of England. The fifty white, five-pointed stars stand for the fifty states that now make up our nation.

Our flag did not always look like this. After independence from England was declared, the first American flag had only thirteen stars to go with the thirteen stripes. As each new state was added to the country, so was a new star and stripe. But, as the flag began to grow, people realized that there would be many more states joining in the United States, and soon the flag would be too big. So in 1818, the members of Congress voted to return the size of the flag to thirteen stripes and add a star for each new state.

The colors of the flag stand for something, too. Red stands for valor, or having great courage. White stands for purity and a goodness that those who founded the country hoped its people would have. Blue stands for justice and the fair treatment of all people who live under the American flag.

This simple piece of cloth called the flag of the United States is a symbol of what makes our country so special.

The United States Flag

Our Flag

Our flag had 13 stars and stripes when it was first made.

The stars and stripes were arranged like this:

	1
	2
	3
	4
	5
	6
	7

8
9
10
11
12
13

Color the odd-numbered stripes red.

Leave the even-numbered stripes white.

Color the background square for the stars blue.

Leave the stars white.

© 1991 Teacher Created Materials, Inc.   67   #113 Hooray for the USA!

The United States Flag

Our Flag *(cont.)*

As new states became part of the United States, a star and a stripe were to be added on the flag for each new state. Soon people realized that if a star and a stripe were added for each state that joined the country, the flag would get too big!

On this page design a flag with 50 stars and 50 stripes.

#113 Hooray for the USA! 68 © 1991 Teacher Created Materials, Inc.

The United States Flag

Our Flag (cont.)

In 1818, Congress decided that a new star would be added to the flag for each new state. The original 13 stripes would stay the same. Through the years, many different arrangements of stars have been made on the flag.

Work in small groups. Cut out the stars on pages 69 and 70. Using a large piece of blue construction paper as the background field, arrange the stars to represent each of the number of states designated below.

FLAG 1 = 18 states   FLAG 4 = 38 states

FLAG 2 = 25 states   FLAG 5 = 43 states

FLAG 3 = 31 states   FLAG 6 = 50 states

When you and your partners have finished all your flags, choose the arrangement of stars you like best and glue them into place. Share your flags with the rest of your class.

Our Flag

Our Flag (cont.)

#113 Hooray for the USA! 70 © 1991 Teacher Created Materials, Inc.

The United States Flag

My Flag

If you were chosen to design the flag that would be the symbol of your country, what would it look like?

Use construction paper, markers, stars, and any other materials you need to create your flag. Share your finished flag with the class.

MY FLAG!

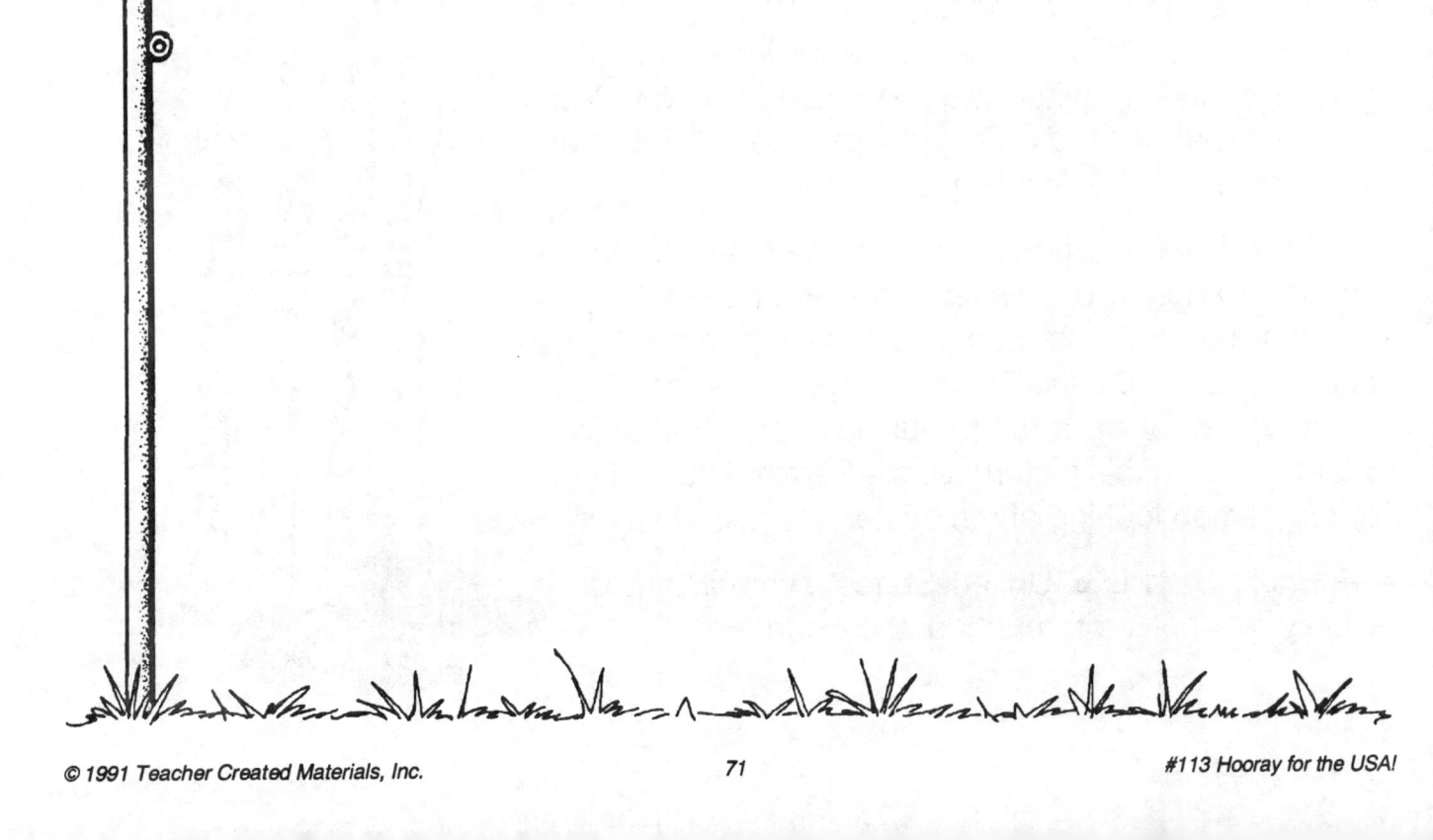

Uncle Sam

Uncle Sam

Who is that tall, bearded man who looks something like an American flag, wearing striped pants, a long tailcoat, and a tall hat covered with stars and stripes? It's Uncle Sam, the figure that has become a symbol of the United States!

There are several stories about the beginning of Uncle Sam, but the one Congress officially recognized in 1961 is the story that follows.

Samuel Wilson was born in Arlington, Massachusetts in 1766. He fought in the Revolutionary War with his father and brothers. When the war was over, he moved to Troy, New York. He started a meatpacking business and was well-respected in his community.

During the War of 1812, Sam Wilson supplied meat to the United States Army in barrels marked U.S. When asked what the U.S. stood for, one of Wilson's workers said, Uncle Sam Wilson, the meatpacker. This story gained popularity when it was printed in a New York City newspaper. Soon many things labeled U.S. were being called Uncle Sam's, not just meat!

After the war, Uncle Sam became a symbol of the nation. People drew him and dressed up like him. A famous cartoonist named Thomas Nast gave him a beard in 1869. During World War I, artist James Flagg painted him for an army recruiting poster that said, "I Want You!" In this picture, Uncle Sam pointed a finger at the person looking at the poster.

Uncle Sam is a United States' symbol that is widely recognized throughout the world.

#113 Hooray for the USA! © 1991 Teacher Created Materials, Inc.

Uncle Sam

Where's My Hat?

Follow these steps to make your own Uncle Sam hat!

You will need these materials for each hat you make:

* a dinner-size paper plate
* a large, cylindrical container such as an oatmeal container
* white stars
* a blue strip of construction paper to fit around the bottom of the container
* a sheet of red construction paper
* a sheet of white construction paper
* a 2 foot length of red, white, or blue yarn

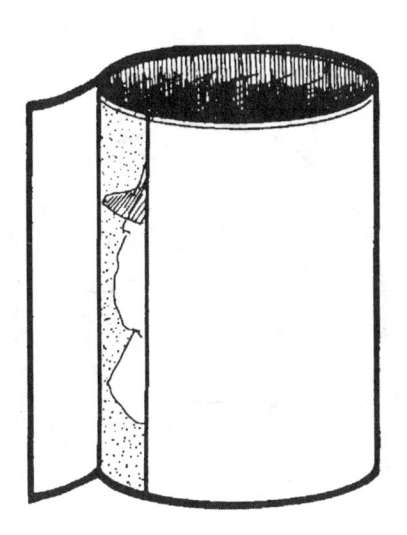

1. Cover the sides of your container with white construction paper. Attach with glue, tape, or staples.

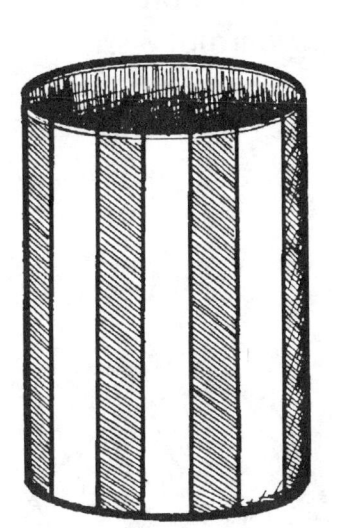

2. Add red construction paper stripes to the white covered part. The stripes should run from top to bottom as shown. Attach with glue, tape, or staples.

3. Cover the bottom of the container with a red construction paper circle. Leave the top uncovered.

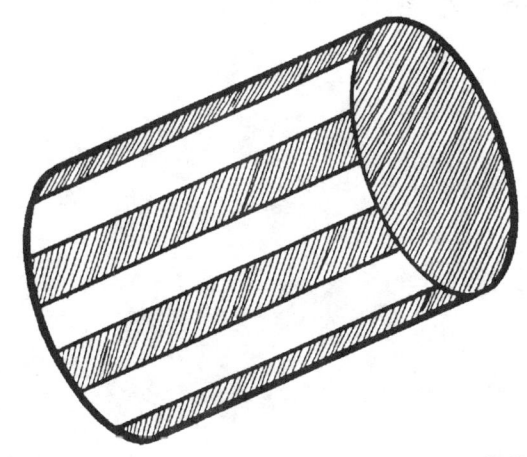

© 1991 Teacher Created Materials, Inc.   73   #113 Hooray for the USA!

Uncle Sam

Where's My Hat? (cont.)

4. Trace the container's opening on the paper plate to make the hat brim.

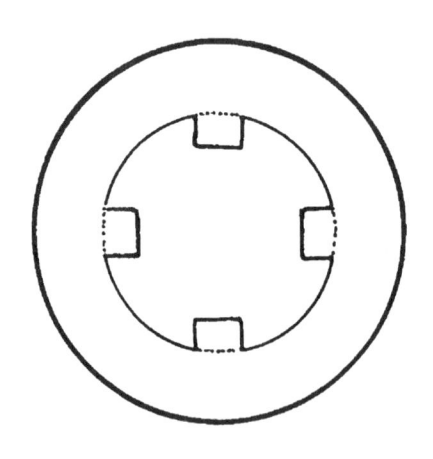

5. Add 4 tabs on the inside of the circle drawn on the plate. Cut out the hat brim, being careful not to cut off the tabs.

6. Attach the hat brim to the container's opening, taping or stapling the tabs to the inside of the container.

#113 Hooray for the USA! © 1991 Teacher Created Materials, Inc.

Uncle Sam

Where's My Hat? (cont.)

7. Measure a blue strip of construction paper to fit around the container, just above the hat brim. Attach it with glue or tape.

8. Decorate the blue strip with white stars. (A pattern for stars can be found on page 70 of this book.)

9. Poke a small hole on opposite sides of the brim.

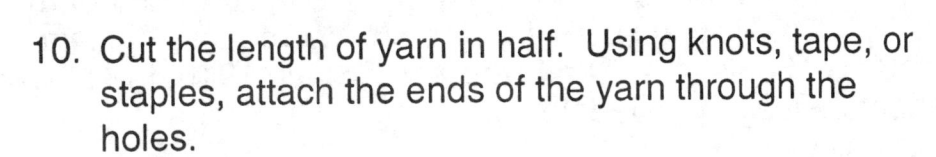

10. Cut the length of yarn in half. Using knots, tape, or staples, attach the ends of the yarn through the holes.

   Tie your Uncle Sam hat under your chin and wear it proudly!

© 1991 Teacher Created Materials, Inc. #113 Hooray for the USA!

The Liberty Bell

On July 8, 1776, a bell rang out to announce the first reading of The Declaration of Independence to the people of Philadelphia. It became then, and still is, a symbol of American Independence.

The people of Pennsylvania sent an order to England in 1751 for the making of a "bell of about two thousand pounds weight" to be used in the State House in Philadelphia. They asked that this inscription be cast around the bell's crown:

"Proclaim Liberty throughout all the land unto all the inhabitants thereof."

Soon after the bell's arrival to America in 1752, it cracked the first time it rang. It was then recast in Philadelphia and began its ringing for freedom. The Old State House Bell, as it was called, was beginning to live up to the words "Proclaim Liberty" that were inscribed on it, even before the people of the New World knew that it was complete liberty they wanted.

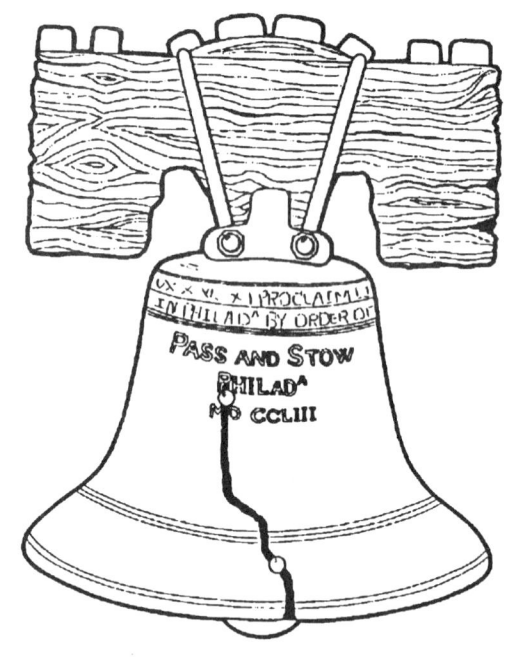

The Old State House Bell rang to summon people to protests of the Stamp Act, the tea tax, and the closing of the port of Boston, as well as to pledge Boston aid. It rang at the public reading of the Declaration of Independence, the Proclamation of Peace with England, and the adoption of the Constitution of the United States. It tolled at the deaths of many important leaders of the fight for democracy. This historic bell rang to proclaim liberty until 1835, when it cracked while tolling during the funeral services of Chief Justice John Marshall.

This bell was known by several names besides the Old State House Bell. It was called the Bell of the Revolution and Old Independence. But it was not until 1839 that it was called the Liberty Bell. An antislavery pamphlet published in this year used the inscription on the great bell as part of its campaign to end slavery: to guarantee freedom "unto all the inhabitants thereof." The pamphlet was called *The Liberty Bell*. The name caught on.

The Liberty Bell became a symbol of freedom, even though it could not be heard. It began to tour the country by train, visiting such places as New Orleans, Chicago, Charleston, Boston, Atlanta, St. Louis, and San Francisco. Since 1915, the Liberty Bell has been on permanent display in Philadelphia.

The Liberty Bell continues to "Proclaim Liberty throughout all the land" and to people throughout the world.

The Liberty Bell

Let Freedom Ring!

On the next three pages, you will find pieces of the Liberty Bell. It is your job to put the pieces together to make our special symbol of freedom.

Once you've put the pieces together, glue or paste the completed bell on a large sheet of construction paper. Use it as the cover for a story about what the Liberty Bell has meant and continues to mean to the people of the United States.

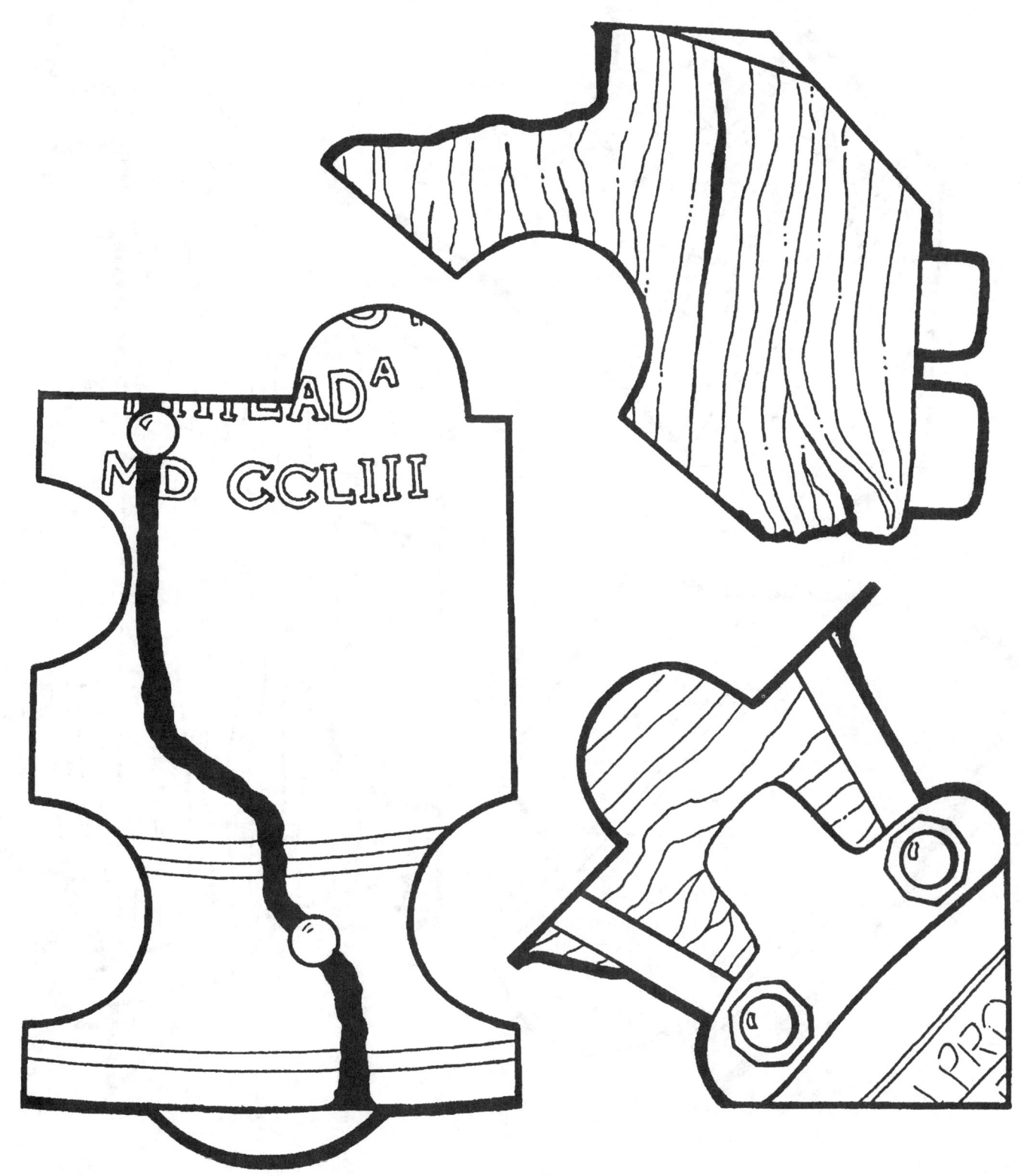

© 1991 Teacher Created Materials, Inc. 77 #113 Hooray for the USA!

The Liberty Bell

Let Freedom Ring! *(cont.)*

Put the pieces of the Liberty Bell together.

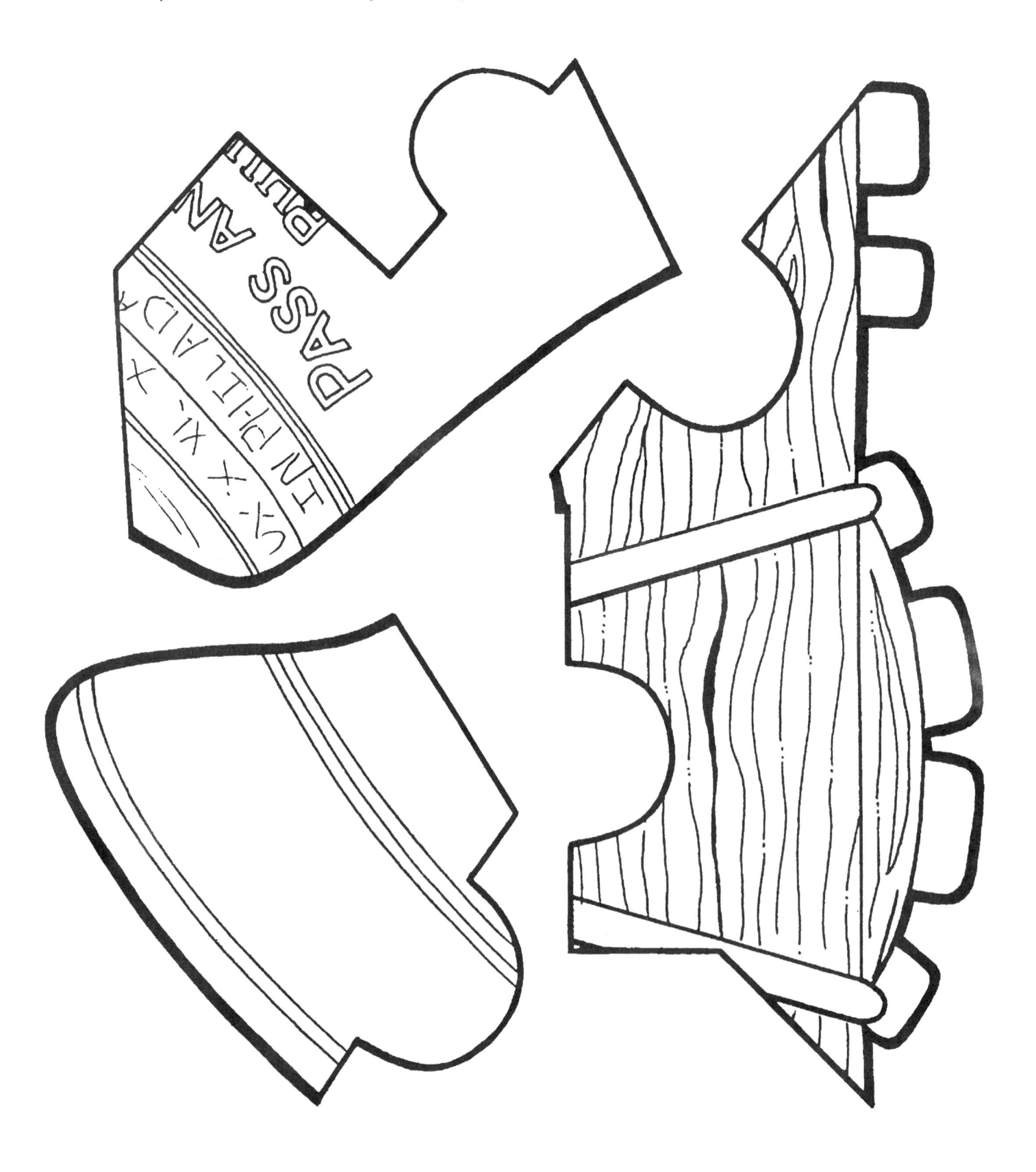

#113 Hooray for the USA! 78 © 1991 Teacher Created Materials, Inc.

The Liberty Bell

Let Freedom Ring! *(cont.)*

Put the remaining pieces of the Liberty Bell together.

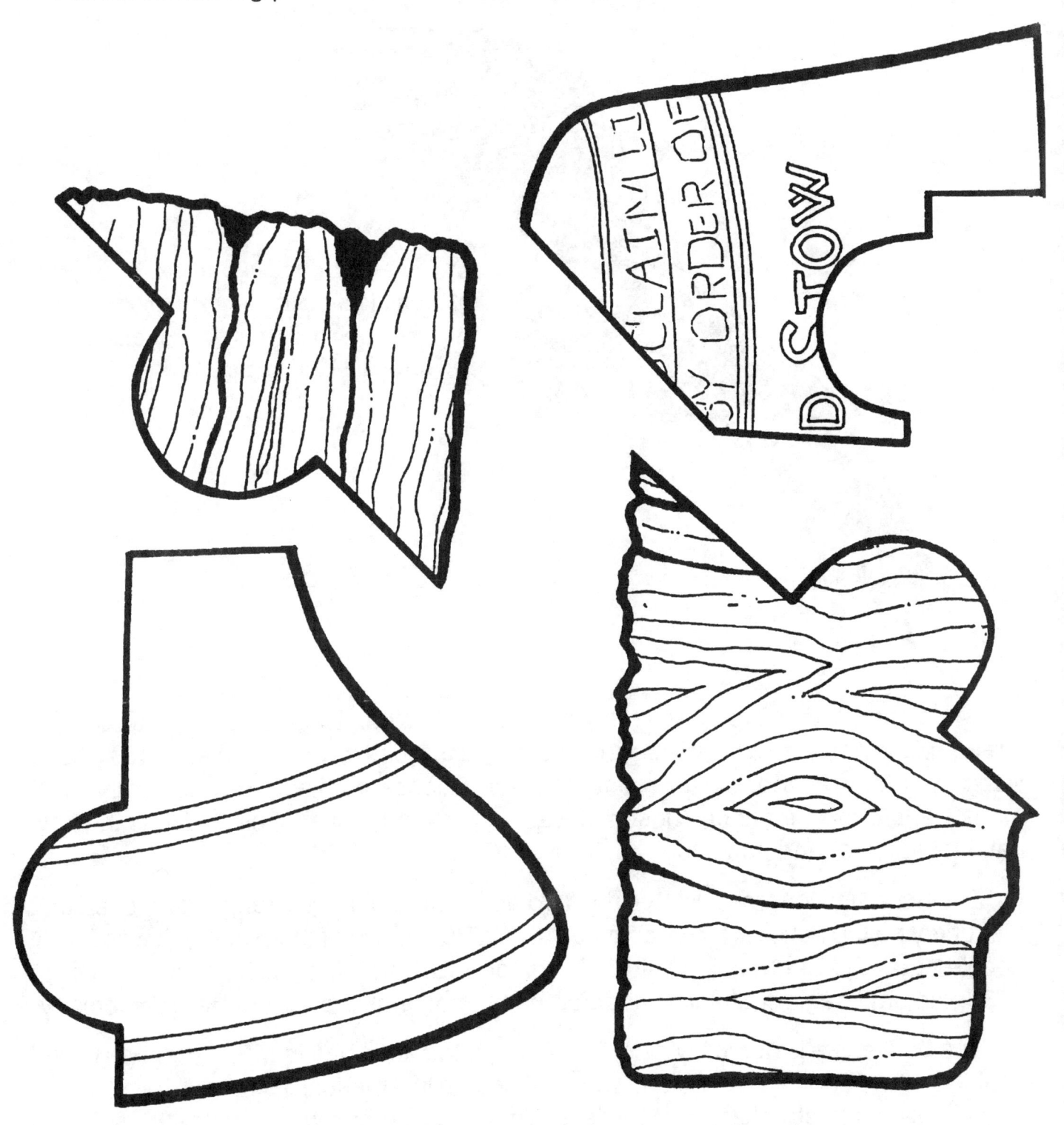

© 1991 Teacher Created Materials, Inc. #113 Hooray for the USA!

The Bald Eagle

This magnificient bird can be found on many things in the United States. It is our national bird, the bald eagle.

Since ancient times, eagles have been a sign of power. Eagles have great size and strength, and because of this, many have claimed this bird as their emblem and symbol. When it came to choosing a national bird for America after the Revolutionary War, many wanted this bird to be chosen. It was a great and powerful bird, just as the new nation was great and powerful.

But, not all in Congress wanted this bird as theirs. Benjamin Franklin proposed that the turkey be the national bird, because it was a true native of the country. It was finally decided that the bald eagle, which was unique to North America, be the choice. In 1782, the bald eagle was finally adopted as the national bird for our new democracy.

The bald eagle is not really bald. The head of the adult bird is white, and was called "bald" by the people from England who first settled in America. To them, "bald" meant "white" or "white-streaked," not hairless! This bird also has white tail feathers.

The bald eagle still serves as our national bird, a symbol of the size and strength of our nation.

The Bald Eagle

Our National Bird

The bald eagle on our dollar bill holds an olive branch in its right talon. The olive branch is a symbol of peace. In its left talon, the eagle holds arrows as a symbol of strength. To make a bald eagle, follow the directions to color, cut out, and assemble the pieces on pages 81-84.

Here is one of the bald eagle's wings and the olive branch.

Color the wing feathers brown with streaks of black.

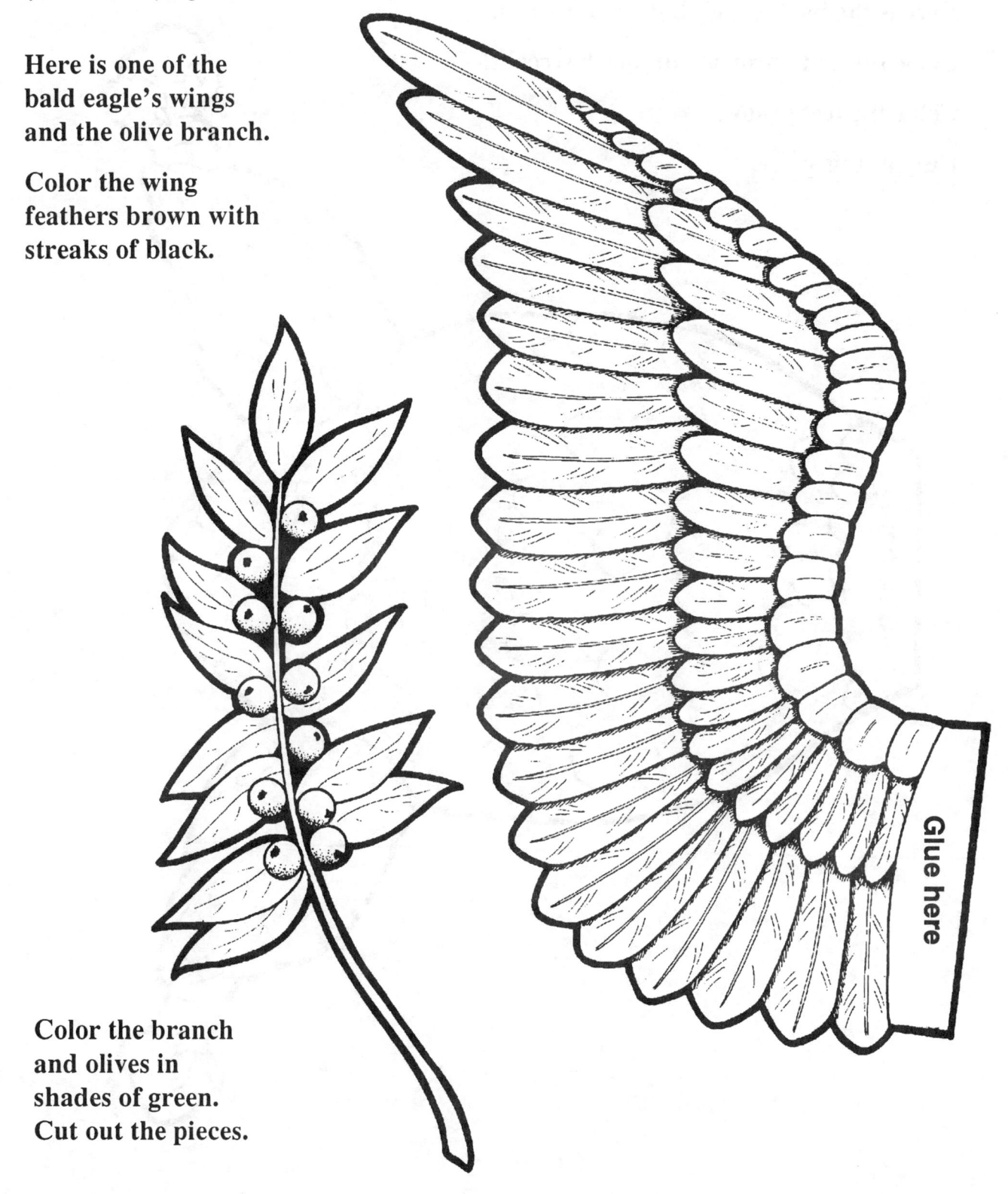

Color the branch and olives in shades of green. Cut out the pieces.

Glue here

© 1991 Teacher Created Materials, Inc.   81   #113 Hooray for the USA!

The Bald Eagle

Our National Bird (cont.)

Use these pattern pieces to make a bald eagle.

Here is the bald eagle's body and its feet.

Color the body brown with black streaks.

Color the feet yellow.

Cut out this piece.

Glue here

The Bald Eagle

Our National Bird (cont.)

Use these pattern pieces to make a bald eagle.

Here are the arrows and the other wing. Color the wing feathers brown with streaks of black. Color the arrows yellow. Cut them out.

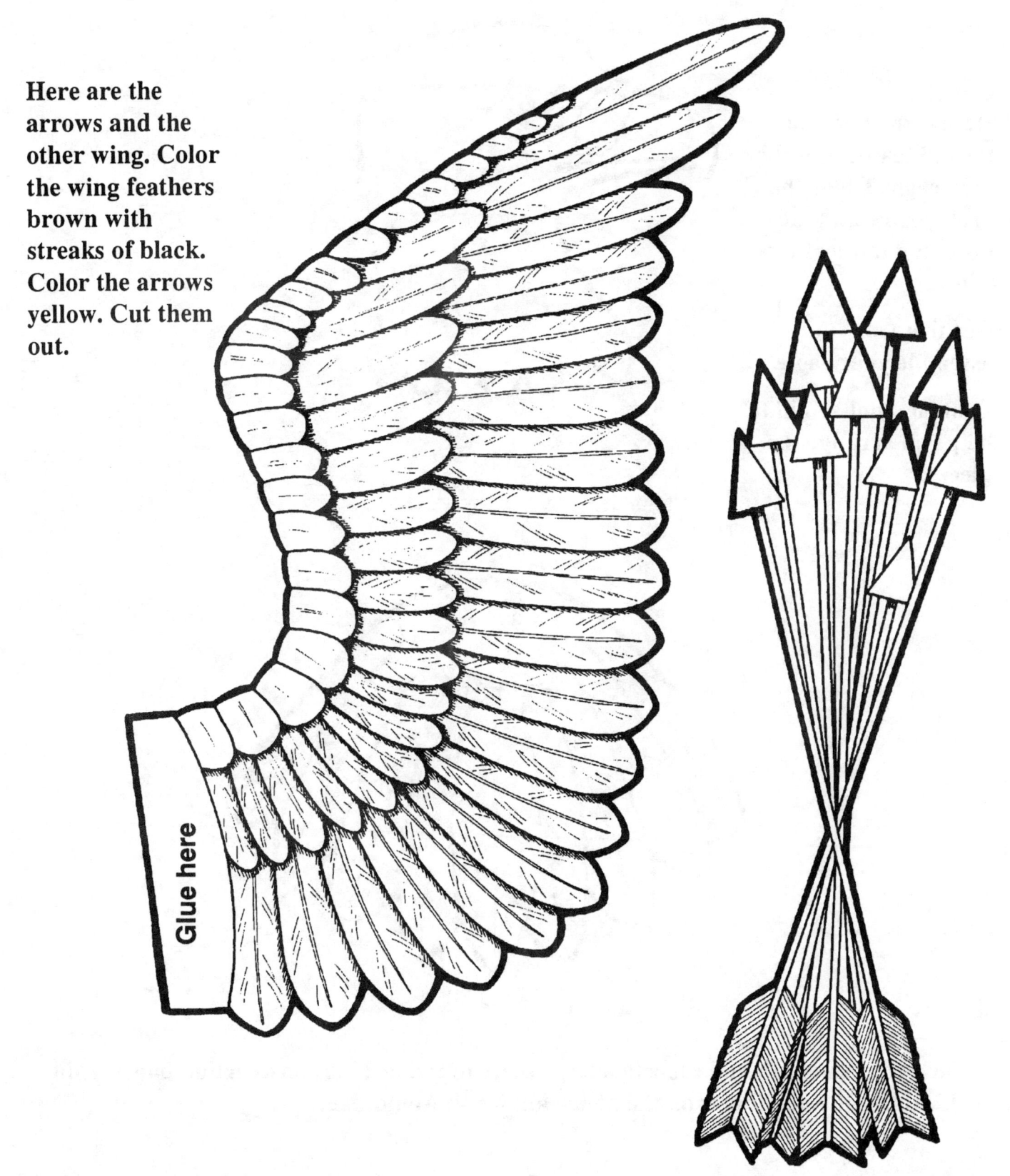

Glue here

The Bald Eagle

Our National Bird (cont.)

Use these pattern pieces to make a bald eagle.

Here is the head and the tail feathers of the bald eagle. Color the beak yellow and the head and tail feathers white.

Cut them out and assemble your eagle.

Look at a dollar bill to help you arrange the pieces.

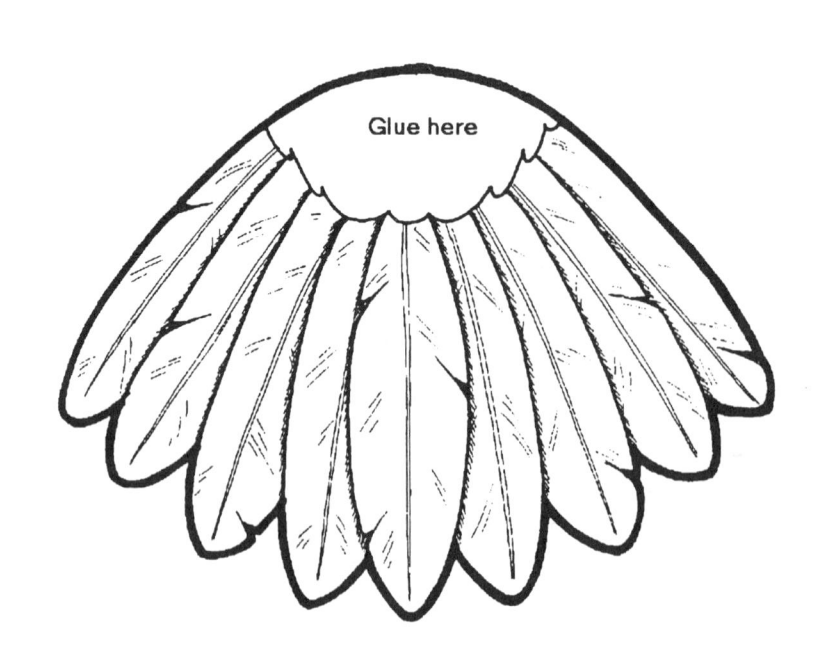

Glue here

Attach your finished bald eagle to a large piece of red or blue construction paper. Add a shield like the one that is on the dollar bill if you would like!

#113 Hooray for the USA! 84 © 1991 Teacher Created Materials, Inc.

The White House

The White House

The most famous house in America can be found at 1600 Pennsylvania Avenue in Washington, D.C. It is the White House, where the President of the United States lives and works.

The White House is the oldest government building in Washington. In 1789, the population center of the new United States was chosen and named the District of Columbia. It was to be a government center and a "Federal City." The first building to be constructed in this new center was to be the home and office of the President. Work began in 1792 on the design by James Hoban.

The building of the President's house took eight years and when it was finished, George Washington was no longer President. The first residents were John and Abigail Adams, the second President and his wife. It was called the Presidential Palace. Thomas Jefferson changed the name of the house to the President's House when he lived there as the nation's third President.

In 1814, during the time of the War of 1812, British soldiers set fire to the President's House. When the fire was finally put out, all that was left standing were the outside walls. After the house was rebuilt, the outside walls were painted white to cover up the fire's black marks. From this time on, it was known as the White House.

Through the years, many changes have been made to the White House. Stately porches, terraces, and wings have been added. The entire structure was strengthened with concrete and steel in the years from 1948 to 1952. In 1961, Mrs. Jacqueline Kennedy, wife of President John F. Kennedy, helped form the White House Historical Association with the purpose of bringing back some of the original White House furnishings and historical contents.

The White House is filled with history and tradition. It is nearly as old as our country itself, and a symbol of American pride. This is one home that belongs to the entire nation.

The White House

The Floor Plan

The rooms in the White House are very famous, and each of these room has a different design and use.

On the following pages are pictures of the floor plans of the White House. Use research materials to correctly label the parts or rooms and their use.

Label these parts of the White House shown in the top view drawn below. On the back of this paper, explain for what each part is used.

Executive Wing	Press Conference Area	President's Office
Theater	East Wing	Main Building

1. _____
2. _____
3. _____
4. _____
5. _____
6. _____

Answer Key: (Cover before duplicating.) 1) East Wing 2) Theater 3) Main Building 4) Press Conference Area 5) President's Office 6) Executive Wing

#113 Hooray for the USA! 86 © 1991 Teacher Created Materials, Inc.

The White House

The Floor Plan (cont.)

Use research materials to label correctly the rooms of the White House shown in this view of the ground floor. On the back of this paper, explain each room's use.

| Diplomatic Reception Room | Vermeil Room | Map Room |
| Ground Floor Corridor | Library | China Room |

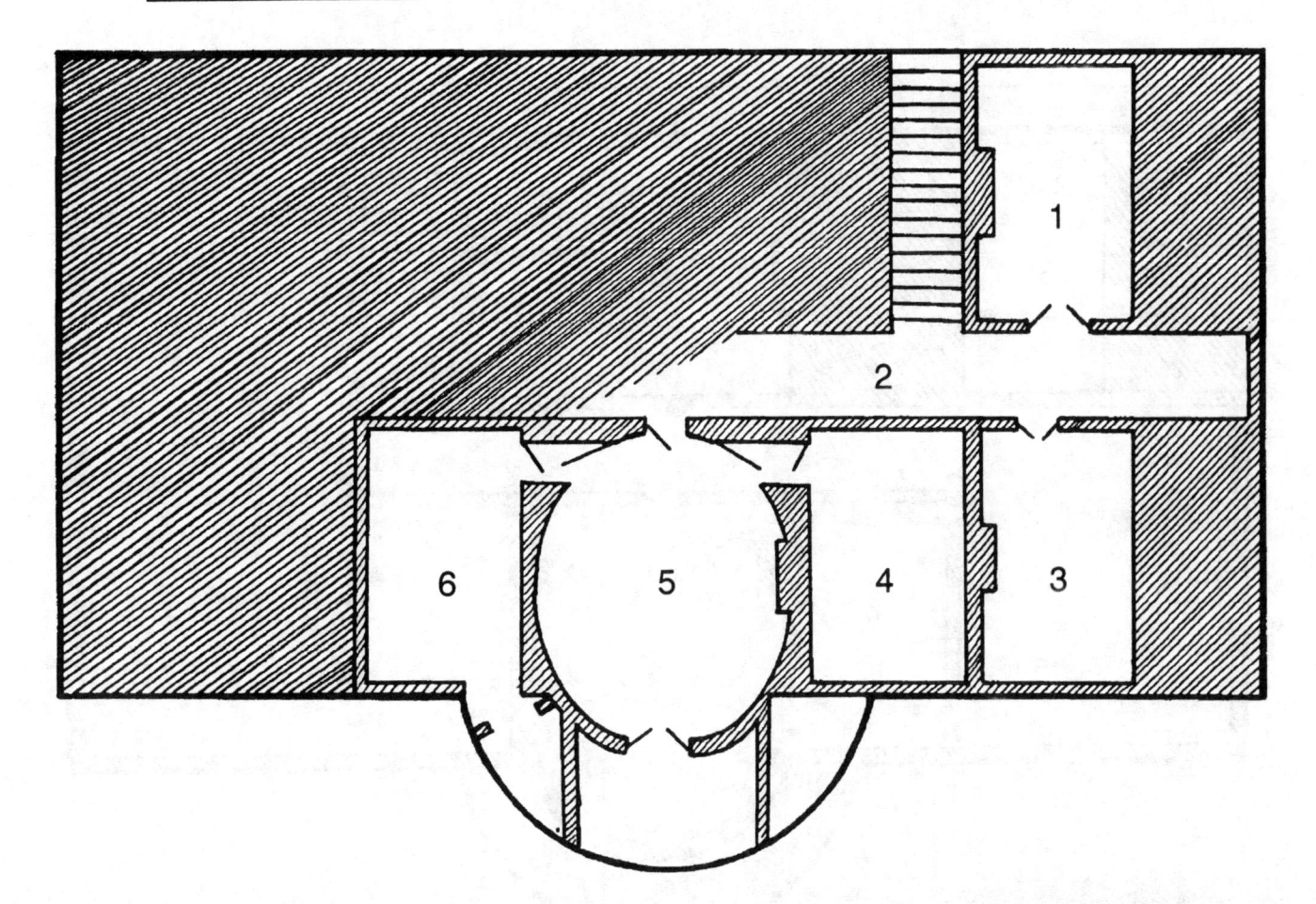

1. _____ 2. _____ 3. _____

4. _____ 5. _____ 6. _____

Answer Key: (Cover before duplicating.) 1) Library   2) Ground Floor Corridor
3) Vermeil Room   4) China Room   5) Diplomatic Reception Room
6) Map Room

© 1991 Teacher Created Materials, Inc.   87   #113 Hooray for the USA!

The White House

The Floor Plan (cont.)

Use research materials to label correctly the rooms of the White House shown in this view of the first floor. On the back of this paper, explain each room's use.

| State Dining Room | Red Room | Entrance Hall | East Room |
| Family Dining Room | Green Room | Cross Hall | Blue Room |

1. _____ 2. _____ 3. _____

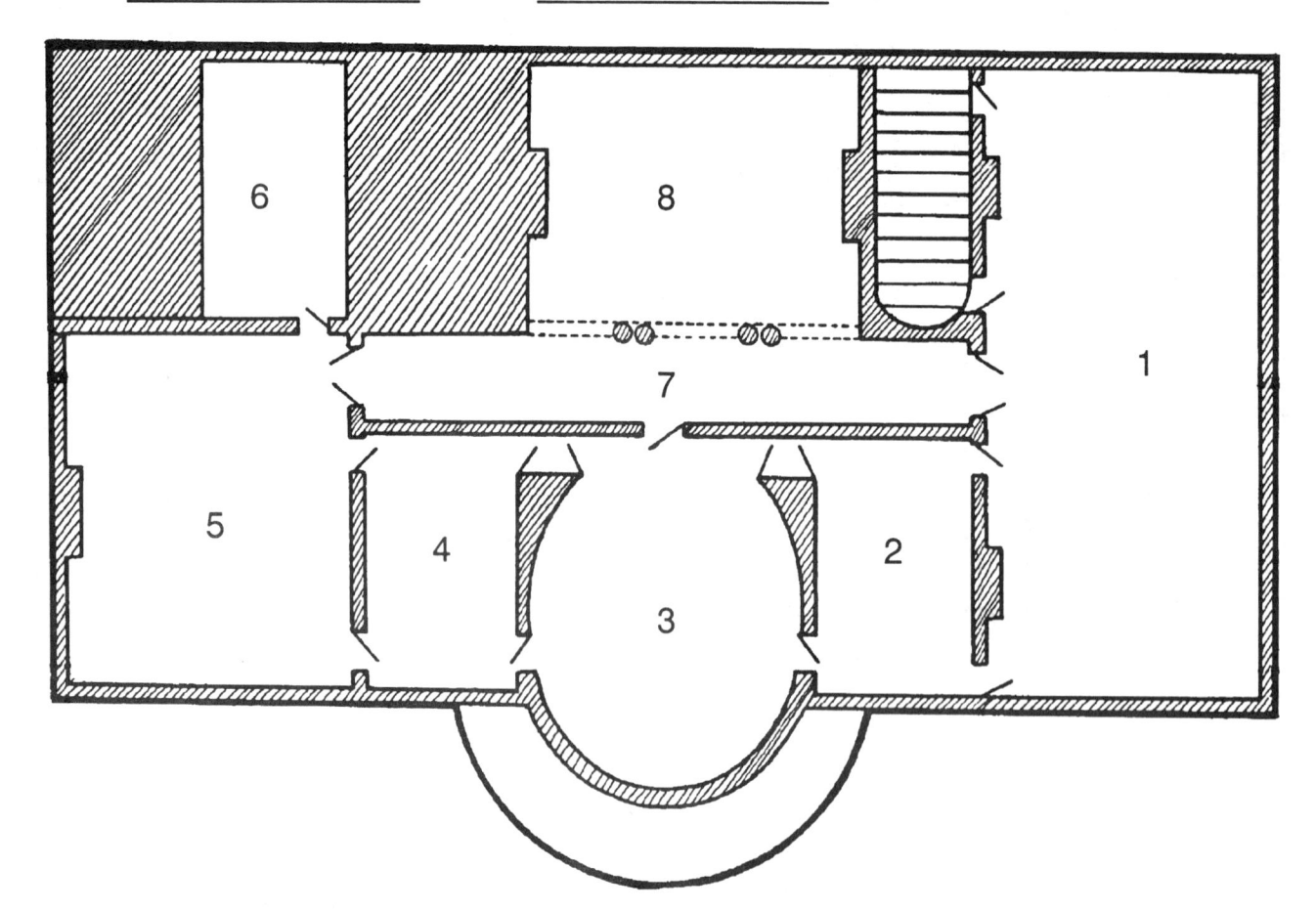

4. _____ 5. _____ 6. _____

7. _____ 8. _____

Answer Key: (Cover before duplicating.) 1) East Room   2) Green Room
3) Blue Room   4) Red Room   5) State Dining Room   6) Family Dining Room
7) Cross Hall   8) Entrance Hall

#113 Hooray for the USA! 88 © 1991 Teacher Created Materials, Inc.

The White House

The Floor Plan (cont.)

Use research materials to label correctly the rooms of the White House shown in this view of the second floor. On the back of this paper, explain each room's use.

| Treaty Room | Queen's Room | Lincoln Bedroom |

1. _____ 2. _____ 3. _____

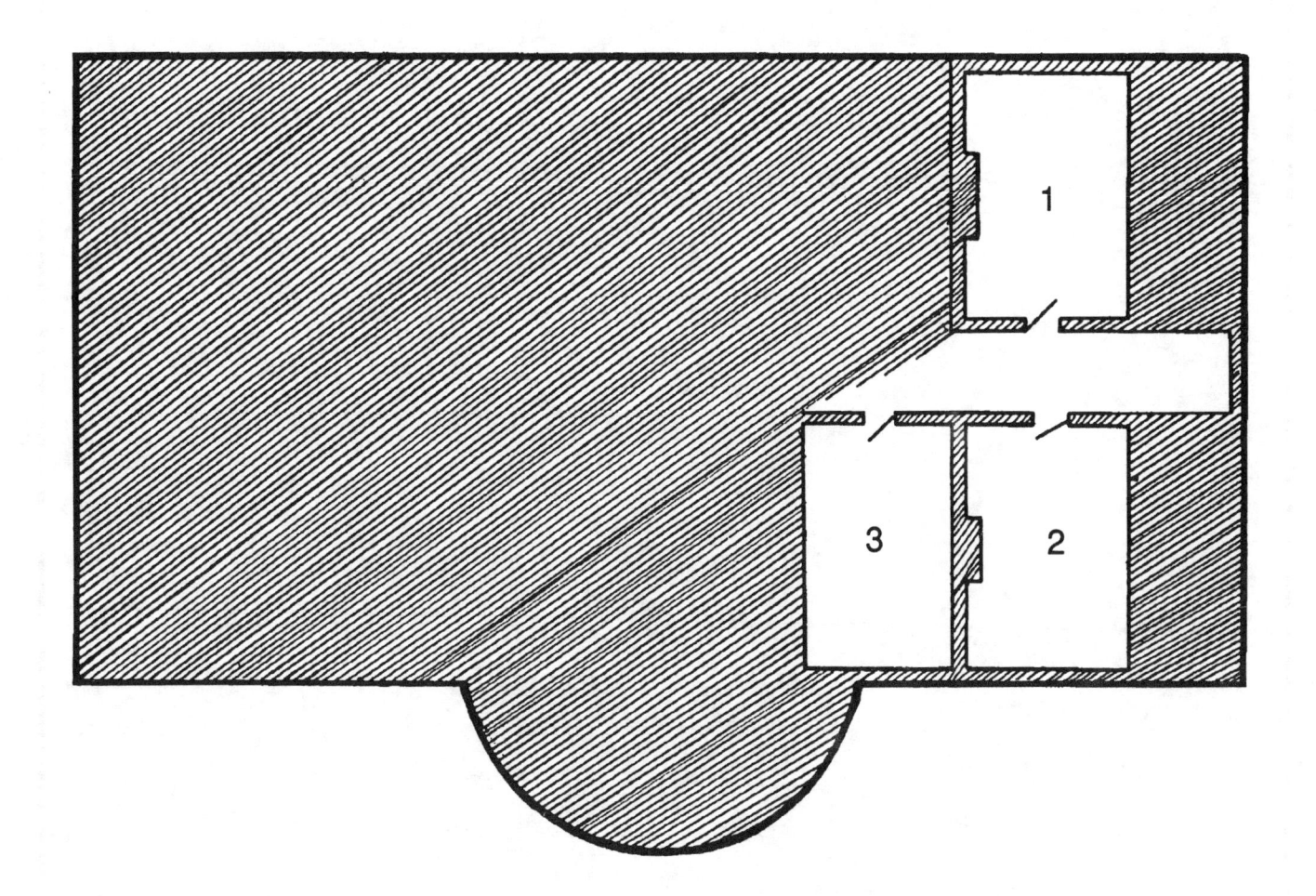

Answer Key: (Cover before duplicating.) 1) Queen's Room   2) Lincoln Bedroom
3) Treaty Room

© 1991 Teacher Created Materials, Inc.   89   #113 Hooray for the USA!

The White House

Your Floor Plan

On this page, design your own floor plan for the perfect Presidential house. With your floor plan, include three papers written on the following areas:

1. Explain the use of each of the areas on your plan.
2. List the similarities and differences between your White House and the existing one.
3. Write an explanation of why your plan is so right for the President!

The United States Capitol

There is a magnificent building that stands on Capitol Hill in Washington, D.C. It is a building to which many people come each year to experience a part of history. This building, the United States Capitol, is not only the seat of the country's government, but a powerful symbol of the democracy on which our nation is based.

In 1793, the cornerstone for the building that was to become the Capitol was laid by President George Washington. Congress met for the first time in the Capitol in 1800. A second similarly-shaped building was built and connected to the first by a wooden passageway before the War of 1812. But when the British stormed Washington, D.C. and burned the White House in 1814, they also set fire to the Capitol, the seat of what they called "Yankee Democracy."

The Capitol had to be rebuilt. This time the wing for the members of the Senate and the wing for the members of the House of Representatives were connected by a building covered by a low dome. But as the nation grew, the building became so crowded that Congress voted to enlarge the wings and make a new, higher, cast-iron dome over the connecting building. On December 2, 1863, in the midst of the Civil War, the Capitol building was finished and topped with a 19 1/2 foot (5.9 meters) bronze statue, the Statue of Freedom.

Inside the Capitol are hundreds of rooms, many of which contain historical collections and famous paintings and sculptures. One entire hall, Statuary Hall, exhibits statues of outstanding Americans chosen from each state. The circular space under the dome is called the Rotunda. Covering its ceiling is a huge fresco painting that glorifies George Washington. People who visit the Capitol may also attend sessions of Congress if they get a pass from one of their representatives in Congress.

The United States Capitol is a building filled with history, beauty, and the power of democracy.

The United States Capitol

Democracy in Action!

In a democracy, a nation is ruled by the people who are in it. In the United States, the needs and opinions of the people who live within its boundaries are heard through the voices of their elected representatives to Congress. The men and women of the Senate and the House of Representatives work hard to understand the concerns and desires of those they are elected to represent. The United States Capitol is the seat of this democratic government.

In this activity, you and your classmates will have a chance to experience democracy in the classroom. First, complete both pages of the following questionnaire. Next, graph the results. Then, compare responses and consolidate similar ideas. Finally, work together to arrive at a classroom program that reflects the desires of the members of the class.

QUESTIONNAIRE FOR A DEMOCRACY, page 1

Name three things about your school or classroom that you would like to see changed. Write them in the order of preference, with the most needed change first on your list.

1. _____
2. _____
3. _____

Name three things about your school or classroom that you would not like to see changed. Write them in the order of preference, with the thing you most want to remain unchanged first.

1. _____
2. _____
3. _____

Are you happy with the seating arrangement in your class? If not, describe how it could be changed to make you happy.

_____
_____
_____

#113 Hooray for the USA!   92   © 1991 Teacher Created Materials, Inc.

The United States Capitol

Democracy in Action! (cont.)

Continue completing the questionnaire. When your class has finished, graph the results of the questionnaire on the board. Work as a class to see how many of the changes wanted by the majority of the people could be implemented. If they can be, try them! If it is not possible, be sure to discuss the reasons why!

QUESTIONNAIRE FOR A DEMOCRACY, page 2

List the subjects you study in school.

1. _____   6. _____
2. _____   7. _____
3. _____   8. _____
4. _____   9. _____
5. _____   10. _____

Understanding that you still need to study all the subjects on the list above, make a schedule of the time of day and the length of time per day you would like to study each.

TIME OF DAY	SUBJECT	LENGTH OF TIME

List any other concerns on the back of this questionnaire.

The Statue of Liberty

The Statue of Liberty

To many people, the Statue of Liberty is one of America's most cherished symbols. It is the symbol of freedom, a freedom that millions of people have come to America to find. Its story is an interesting one.

The people of France had long admired the liberty enjoyed by the people who lived in the United States. In 1865, Edouard de Laboulaye wanted to give a gift to the United States that would be a tribute to this liberty as well as a symbol of the friendship between the two countries. This idea became a reality when a sculptor named Frederic Auguste Bartholdi sailed to the United States to find support and a location for France's gift. New York's Bedloe Island was chosen as the site and a colossal statue as the gift. The sculptor sailed home to begin work on the monument.

Bartholdi decided to create a huge statue of a robed woman with her right arm holding a torch high above her head. He modeled her face after the strong features of his own mother's face. Construction began on "Lady Liberty" in a Paris workshop in 1875. Funds for the statue were raised by the French people. By July 4, 1876, Bartholdi had completed the right hand and torch and sent it to the United States to display for their centennial celebration of the signing of the Declaration of Independence. At home, the sculptor continued to work on the rest of the statue. He was helped greatly by Alexander Gustave Eiffel, who designed the framework to support the gigantic statue.

Meanwhile, back in the United States, money was being raised for the base and the pedestal necessary to support France's gift. Plans were being made by Richard Morris Hunt for the design. Construction on the pedestal started in 1884 but soon stopped because the money ran out. The needed funds were finally raised because of a newspaper campaign started by Joseph Pulitzer. He appealed to people all over the United States to help in the building of the monument. Pennies, nickels, dimes, and dollars rolled in from all over the country, sent by children as well as adults. In less than five months, the newspaper campaign had helped to raise the needed money. About 121,000 people had given the $100,000 needed to finish the pedestal.

The completed statue was officially presented to the United States in Paris, France on July 4, 1884. It was then carefully taken apart and shipped to America. The statue arrived in 1885 and the pedestal was completed in April of 1886.

Liberty Enlightening the World was dedicated on Bedloe Island on October 28, 1886, over ten years after the work began. Bartholdi was there, as were members of the French government. People of America and the world over were delighted with this special monument.

Major restoration was conducted on the statue in the 1980s and completed in 1986, just in time for a festive celebration to mark the statue's 100th birthday.

The Statue of Liberty

Liberty Enlightening the World

Here are some interesting statistics about the statue:

pedestal height:
    154 feet (47 meters)

statue height:
    151 feet, 1 inch (46.05 meters)

statue weight:
    450,000 pounds (204 metric tons)

combined height:
    305 feet, 1 inch (92.99 meters) from the base of the pedestal to the top of the torch

torch arm:
    32 feet (13 meters)

face:
    10 feet (3 meters) from ear to ear

across each eye:
    2 feet, 6 inches (.8 meters)

The name of Bedloe Island was changed to Liberty Island officially in 1956. Over the years, *Liberty Enlightening the World* has commonly been called The Statue of Liberty. It became a symbol of hope for the millions of immigrants who came by it on their way to settle in America. American poet Emma Lazarus wrote a poem which was placed on a plaque in the pedestal in 1903. The words gave, and continue to give, a message of hope to all who wish to settle in our land of liberty.

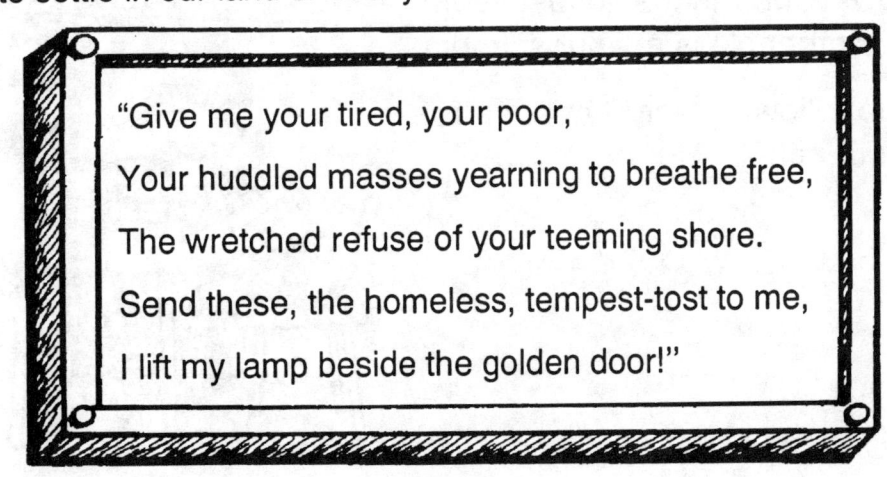

> "Give me your tired, your poor,
>
> Your huddled masses yearning to breathe free,
>
> The wretched refuse of your teeming shore.
>
> Send these, the homeless, tempest-tost to me,
>
> I lift my lamp beside the golden door!"

The Statue of Liberty

Your Symbol!

The Statue of Liberty was given to the United States by France as a symbol of friendship between the two countries.

What kind of gift would you give to show your friendship:

between you and a very good friend? _____
_____

between you and a family member? _____
_____

between your class and another class at your school? _____
_____

between your school and another school in the area in which you live? _____
_____

between your country and another country? _____
_____

between your planet and beings from another planet? _____
_____

As a class project, decide upon a symbol that would show your friendship between your class and another class at your school.

Complete the following activity pages to help you plan your gift.

The Statue of Liberty

Your Symbol! *(cont.)*

The creator of the Statue of Liberty made many designs before he was ready to begin his work.

Draw one or more possible designs for your friendship gift to another class at your school. Add your drawings to a class display. Work together to choose one idea to use from the designs submitted by you and your classmates.

Original Design by _____

The Statue of Liberty

Your Symbol! *(cont.)*

Emma Lazarus wrote a poem called "The New Colossus" which was inscribed on a plaque and attached to the Statue of Liberty pedestal in 1903. In this poem, Lazarus welcomes the immigrants who are searching for freedom in the United States.

Write a poem that expresses the way you feel about the class to whom you are giving the friendship gift. Remember to make them feel good! Submit your poem to the class. Work together to select the poem that best expresses your feelings toward the other class.

_____

by

_____

_____

_____

_____

_____

_____

_____

_____

_____

The Statue of Liberty

Your Symbol! *(cont.)*

The celebration that welcomed *Liberty Enlightening the World* to New York Harbor was a grand and festive one.

Work as a class to plan a ceremony to give your gift of friendship to the other class at your school.

Include these things in your plans:

        a news release   an invitation

        a program   ceremony notes

Here is an outline you can use to prepare your ceremony notes.

CEREMONY NOTES

Date: _____ Time: _____

Location: _____

Special Invited Guests:

_____ _____

_____ _____

_____ _____

Opening Ceremony: _____

Music: _____

Speakers:

_____ _____

_____ _____

Special Presentations:

_____

                              presented by _____

_____

                              presented by _____

Closing Ceremony: _____

Ellis Island

For hundreds of years, people from other countries have come to the United States seeking the freedom that is possible in this land of promise. Over 80% of these immigrants have made their way to America by way of New York City.

Ellis Island, near Liberty Island in New York Harbor, served as an immigration station for over 60 years, screening over 12 million immigrants. It opened as a reception center in 1892. In 1897, the wooden buildings burned and were replaced by a castle-like, beautiful structure in 1900. This structure was used to process immigrants until 1943, when New York City took on these duties.

During World War II, Ellis Island was a special type of "immigration" center, one that served as a detention center for illegal or criminal aliens who were in the United States. The Coast Guard also had some training programs there. In 1954 Ellis Island was closed. Over the years, the structures there became ruined by time and vandalism.

Ellis Island became part of the Statue of Liberty National Monument in 1965. Beginning in the 1980s, a gigantic restoration effort began. Over the years, the original structure and character of Ellis Island has been restored. On Monday, September 10, 1990, The Ellis Island Immigration Museum was opened. In this magnificent museum, exhibits help to recreate the immigrant experience for its many visitors.

Ellis Island

To Be an Immigrant

Immigrants went through several steps once they came to Ellis Island. They entered the main building and checked in their baggage. As they climbed the stairs to the Registry Room, they were given a "six-second medical" and checked for contagious diseases. Those who passed the medical inspection moved on into the Registry Room where their legal documents were checked. They were also asked questions by the inspectors. Those who passed were allowed into the ticket office to buy tickets to the places they wanted to go. Those who were detained were housed in rooms in the main building and fed their meals in the dining room. Only 2% of the immigrants who came to Ellis Island were sent back to their homelands.

What would it be like to be an immigrant to the United States? There are probably people in your family or in your community who have immigrated to this country from other places.

Invite an immigrant to speak to your class about his or her experiences. Here is an interview idea sheet to help you ask questions of your guest.

Name of speaker: _____

Date of entry into the United States: _____

Place of entry into the United States: _____

Here are some questions you might like to ask your guest:

1. Could you give us the name of your homeland and a description of how it was when you left?
2. Why did you leave?
3. Why did you come to the United States?
4. What was your first day in the United States like? What things did you have to do? What questions were you asked? How did you feel?
5. Who did you know that was living here? Did this person or these people help you in any way?
6. What do you miss about your homeland?
7. What do you like and dislike about the United States?
8. Would you ever go back to your homeland? Explain.

Famous Memorials

Famous Memorials

Many memorials have been created for people and events throughout the history of the United States. These memorials honor special times and patriotic Americans. Here are three of the most famous memorials in our country.

The Washington Monument was built in honor of our first President, George Washington. The building of the monument began in 1880 and was completed in 1884. It's obelisk shape rises 555 feet, 5 $\frac{1}{8}$ inches (169.29 meters) above Washington, D.C. The inside of the monument is hollow, with many carved memorial stones set in its inner walls. People can ride an inside elevator to the top of the monument and get a spectacular view of the Washington area.

The Thomas Jefferson Memorial was built in honor of our third President and author of the Declaration of Independence, Thomas Jefferson. Construction of this memorial began in 1938 and was dedicated on the 200th anniversary of his birth, April 13, 1943. A white marble dome tops this beautiful circular building, and a portico, or porch, supported by 12 columns completes the outside design. Inside is a 19 foot (5.8 meters) bronze statue of Jefferson, as well as panels engraved with quotations from his writings.

The Lincoln Memorial honors Abraham Lincoln, the 16th President of the United States. Work on this monument began in 1915 and was completed in 1922. It is a huge, temple-like, white marble building that is 189 feet (58 meters) long and 118 $\frac{2}{3}$ feet (36.2 meters) wide. Thirty-six tall columns support the roof of the building. On the inside is a magnificent marble statue of Lincoln sitting in a chair. Also inside the memorial are tablets with the Gettysburg Address and his Second Inaugural Address, as well as paintings that show Lincoln's role in history.

These three memorials will help us long remember three men who helped to make the United States great.

Famous Memorials

The Washington Monument

Color this picture of the Washington Monument. When you have finished, use page 104 to write a short summary of what Washington did to help make the United States great. Attach it to your picture.

© 1991 Teacher Created Materials, Inc. #113 Hooray for the USA!

Famous Memorials

The Washington Monument (cont.)

Use this profile of Washington for writing your summary of what he did to help make the United States great. Then, attach this page to the page you have colored.

Famous Memorials

The Thomas Jefferson Memorial

Color this picture of the Thomas Jefferson Memorial. When you have finished, use page 106 to write a short summary of what Jefferson did to help make the United States great. Use the profile page writing sheet for your summary. Then, attach it to your colored picture.

Famous Memorials

The Thomas Jefferson Memorial

Use this profile of Jefferson to write your summary of what he did to make the United States great. Attach this page to the page you have colored.

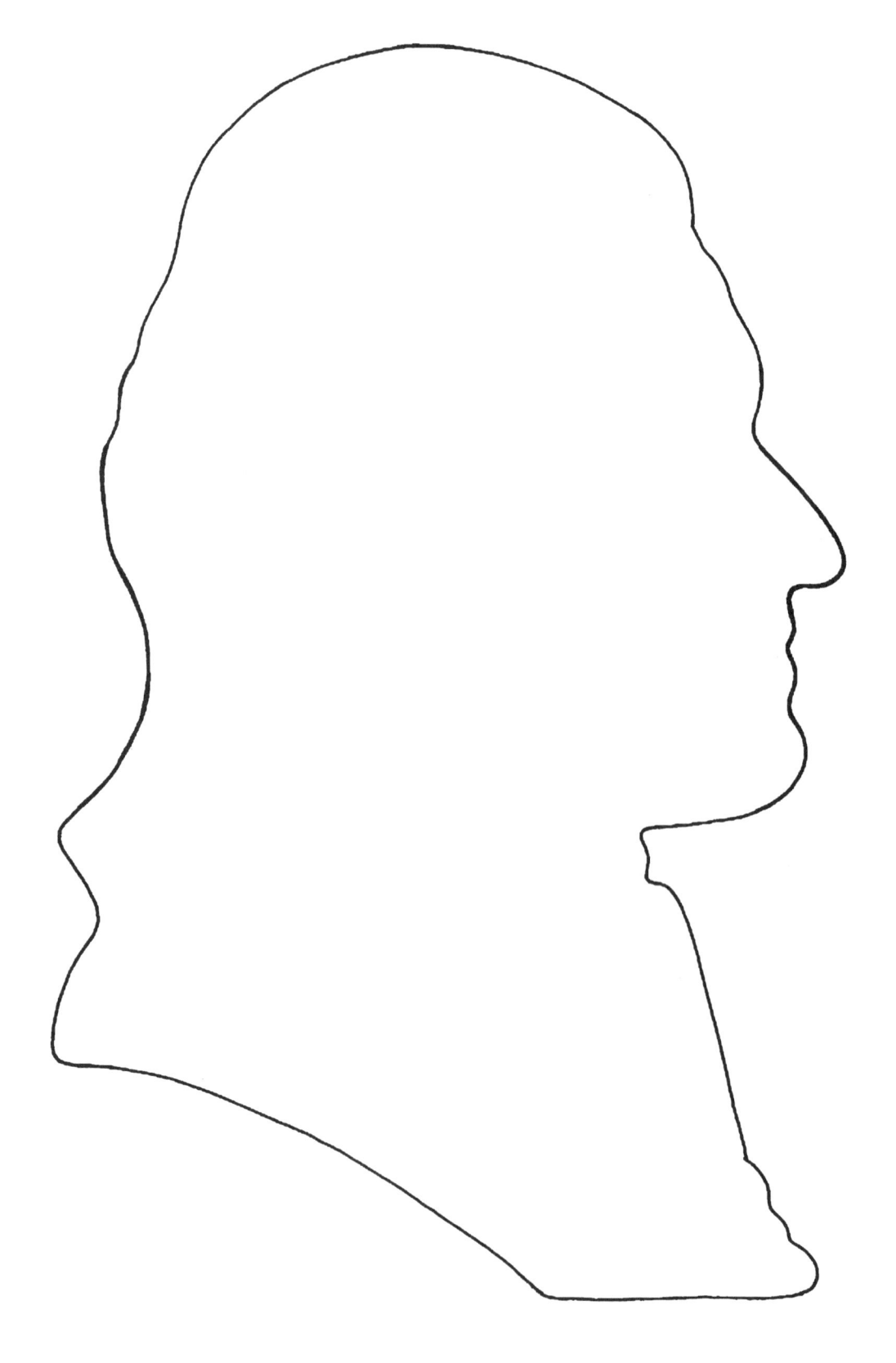

Famous Memorials

The Lincoln Memorial

Color this picture of the statue within the Lincoln Memorial. When you have finished, use page 108 to write a short summary of what Lincoln did to help make the United States great. Then, attach it to your colored picture.

Famous Memorials

The Lincoln Memorial

Use this profile of Lincoln to write your summary of what he did to make the United States great. Then, attach this page to the page you have colored.

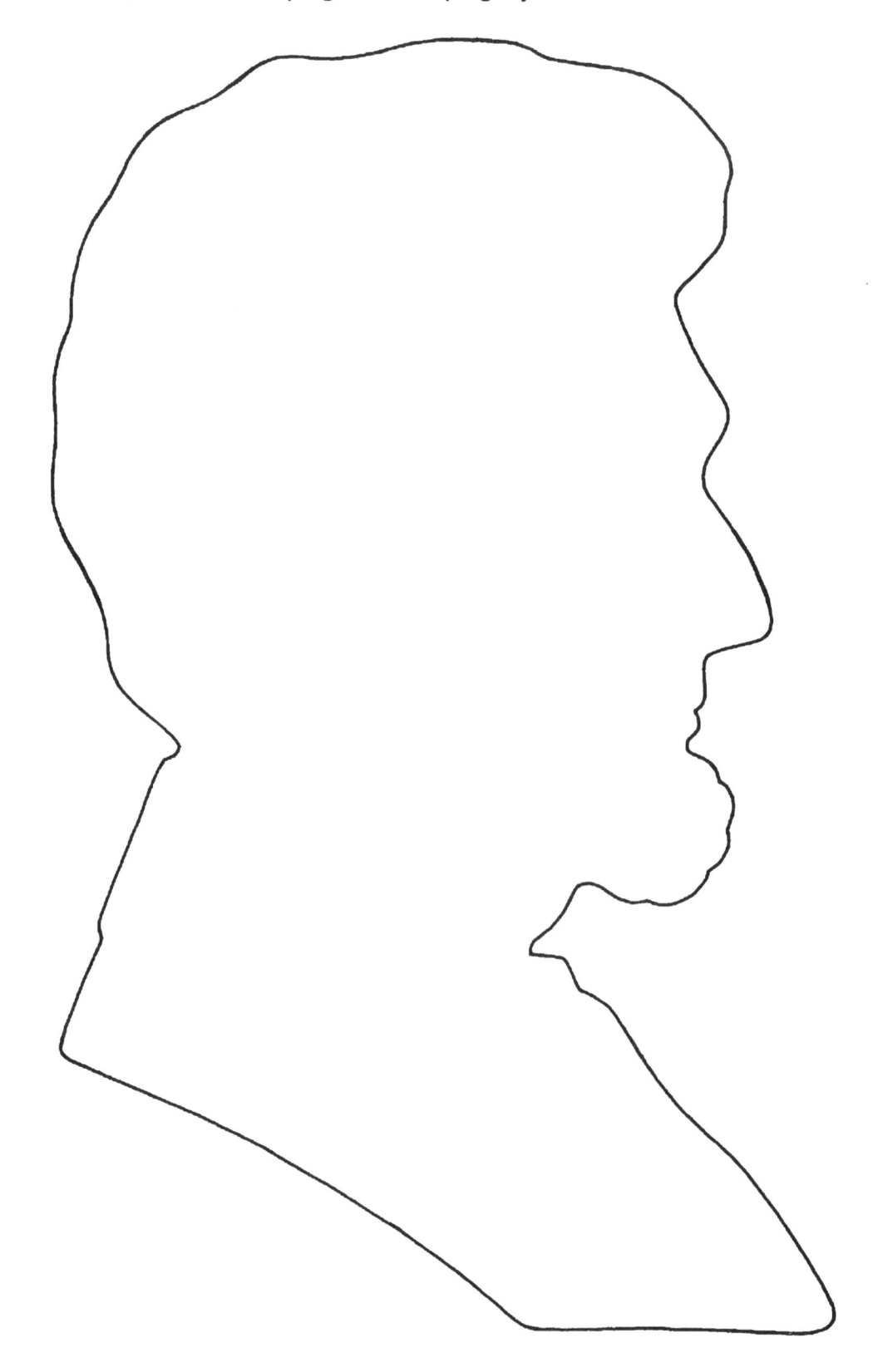

Mount Rushmore

Mount Rushmore

In the Black Hills of South Dakota is a spectacular creation in the granite cliff of Mount Rushmore. It is a carving of four of the Presidents of the United States: George Washington, Thomas Jefferson, Theodore Roosevelt, and Abraham Lincoln. It serves as a memorial to these great men.

Doane Robinson, State Historian of South Dakota in 1923, had the idea of making a gigantic sculpture in the Black Hills. He invited sculptor Gutzon Borglum to the Black Hills to see if such a thing could be done. When Borglum saw the site, he suggested that a memorial to several Presidents be made. Work began on August 10, 1927. On the same day, President Calvin Coolidge declared Mount Rushmore a National Memorial.

Borglum made scale models of the Presidents using 1 inch on the model to 12 inches on the mountain. To transfer his design to the cliff face he used dynamite to remove the extra rock. A hammer, wedging tool, and an air hammer did the fine detail work. After Borglum died in 1941, his son, Lincoln, finished the work. The carving of the Presidents took 14 years.

The Presidents' faces on Mount Rushmore were carved on a scale of a human being 465 feet tall. The faces average 60 feet from chin to top. Each nose is 20 feet, each mouth 18 feet, and each eye 11 feet across.

Each of the Presidents carved into Mount Rushmore symbolizes something that makes America great. Washington stands for the struggle for independence and the birth of our Republic. Jefferson represents the ideal of government of the people, by the people, and for the people. Lincoln symbolizes the struggle for equality, and Roosevelt stands for the conscience and influence of 20th-century America.

Mount Rushmore is a national treasure for us all.

Mount Rushmore

Map the Route

Here is a map of the continental United States. Map the route you would take from where you live to arrive in South Dakota.

Write your travel directions on the back of this page.

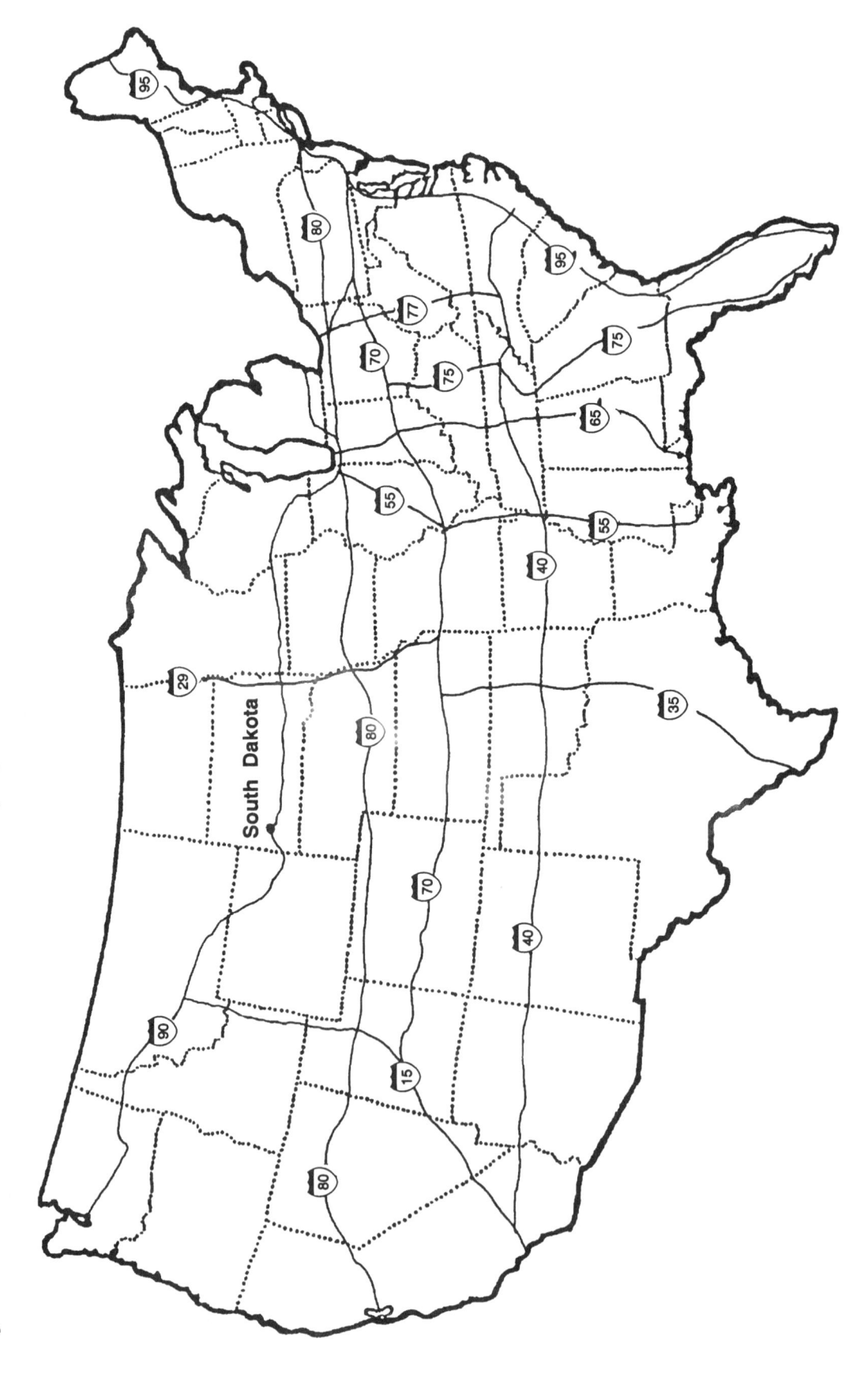

#113 Hooray for the USA! 110 © 1991 Teacher Created Materials, Inc.

Mount Rushmore

Map the Route (cont.)

Here is a map of South Dakota. Map the route you would take from the point you would enter the state to arrive in Rapid City. Using the map legend, determine how many miles it would be from your entry into the state to Rapid City. Also determine how long your journey would take.

Write your travel directions and the miles and time of your trip at the bottom of this page.

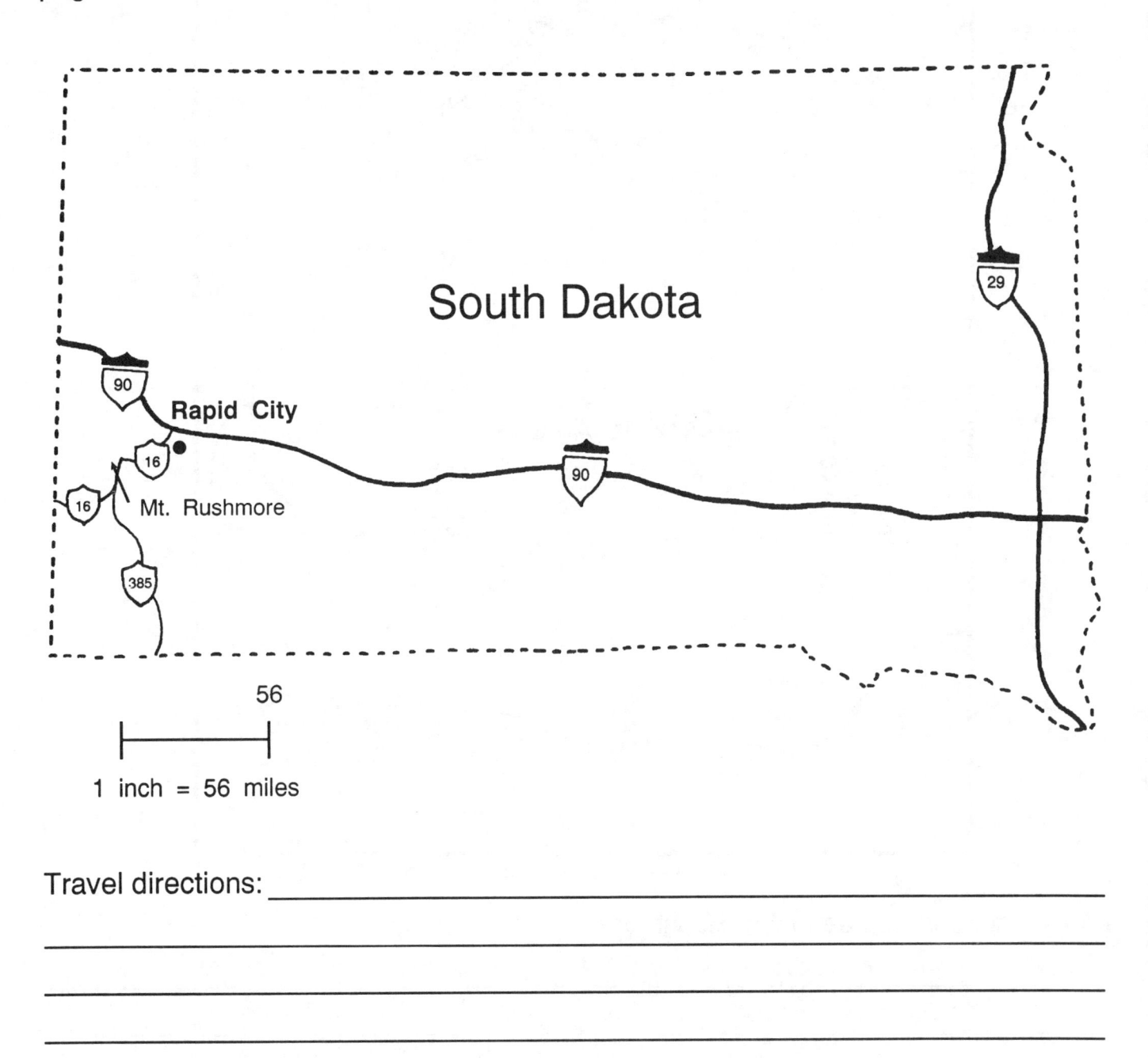

South Dakota

90 Rapid City
16
16 Mt. Rushmore
385
29
90

56
⊢―――⊣
1 inch = 56 miles

Travel directions: _____
_____
_____
_____
_____
_____

Miles traveled: _____ Time of trip: _____

Mount Rushmore

Map the Route (cont.)

Here is a map of the area around Mount Rushmore. Use a colored marker to show your route to Mount Rushmore.

At the bottom of the page, explain why you would like to see Mount Rushmore, and what about the memorial you would find most interesting if you were to get the chance to see it in person.

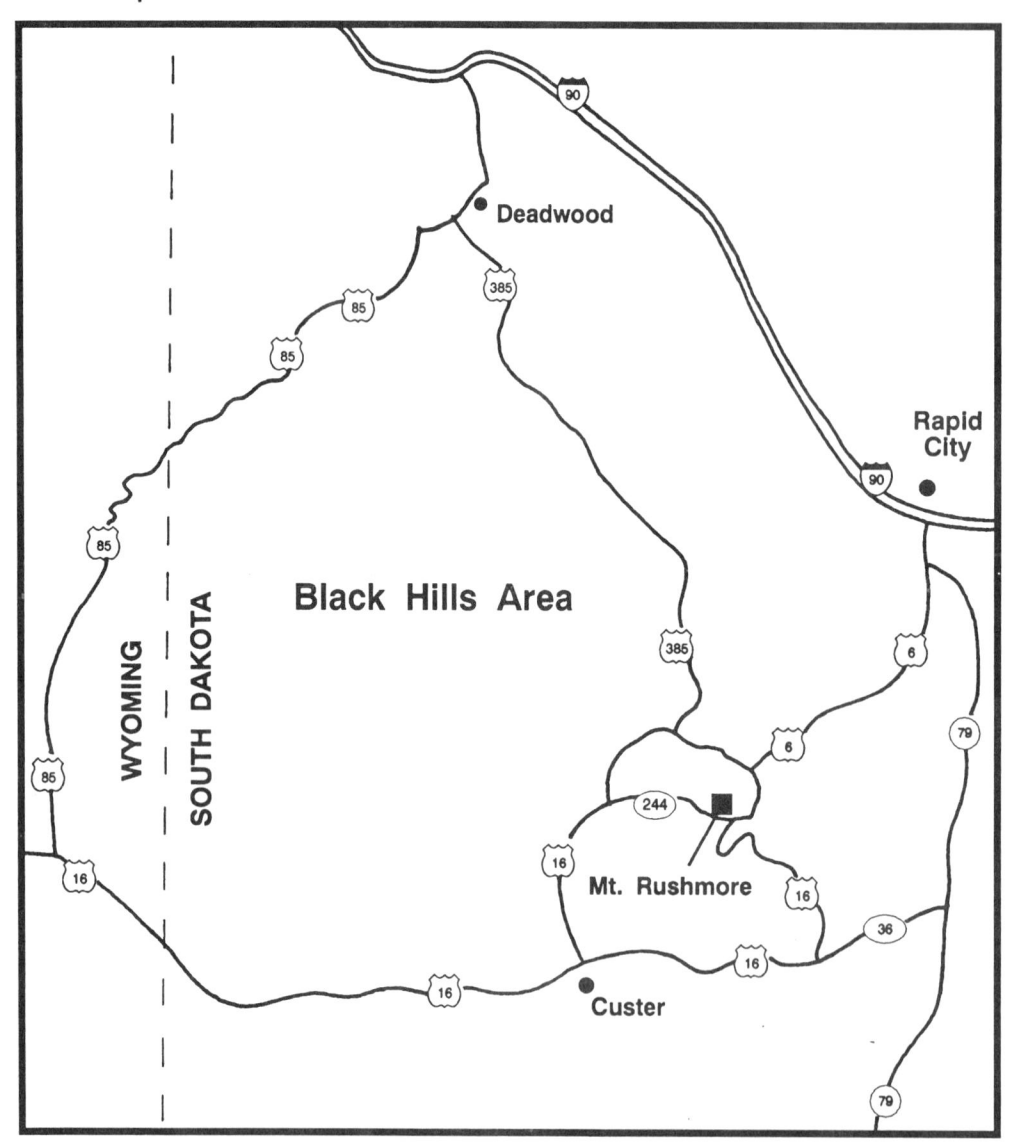

Why I would like to see Mount Rushmore:

_____

_____

What I would find most interesting if I were to see it:

_____

_____

#113 Hooray for the USA! 112 © 1991 Teacher Created Materials, Inc.